Praise for *In All Things... Moral Reflections and Decisions on Life Issues*:

"James Jackson provides great insights on daily living and societal issues, blended nicely with biblical principles."

James Barrett; CEO
Michigan Chamber of Commerce

"Mr. Jackson does an excellent job contrasting basic biblical scripture with modern-day social norms to challenge your spiritual comfort zone."

J. C. Crane, Jr.; Vice-President
Crane Enterprises, Inc

"'English is an open window to the outer world,' said the first Prime Minister of India, Jawaharlal Nehru. I not only read Jim Jackson's articles in English, but also translate and publish them in the magazine *Lutheran Saba* (Lutheran Voice) in Malayalam, the language of Southern India. To every reader Jim's articles open not only windows but doors also. If you are 'shut down inside your own thoughts,' Jim will open the windows and doors. His words are as sharp as the sword and as powerful as the hammer."

Rev. Stanley Lawrence
Passiton, India; Trivandrum, India

"Jim's writings are straight from the heart. His style of pure common sense tells it like it is. Easy to read and right to the point. You can't read one of his articles without uttering 'Amen' at the end!"

Mary Spagnoulo
The Amy Foundation Internet Syndicate

W9-CGL-096

IN ALL THINGS...

Moral Reflections & Decisions on Life Issues

To Kathy,
May this book be a blessing
To you and yours!

Jim

Jim J Garber

IN ALL THINGS...

Moral Reflections & Decisions on Life Issues

ACKNOWLEDGING GOD'S ANSWERS TO DAILY CHALLENGES

James J. Jackson

TATE PUBLISHING *& Enterprises*

Published by Tate Publishing & Enterprises, LLC
127 E. Trade Center Terrace | Mustang, Oklahoma 73064 USA
1.888.361.9473 | www.tatepublishing.com

Tate Publishing is committed to excellence in the publishing industry. The company reflects the philosophy established by the founders, based on Psalm 68:11,
"The Lord gave the word and great was the company of those who published it."

Book design copyright © 2008 by Tate Publishing, LLC. All rights reserved.
Cover design by Elizabeth A. Mason
Interior design by Lynly D. Taylor

Published in the United States of America

ISBN: 978-1-60462-254-6
1. Christian Living: Social Issues/Character and Values

09.04.28

DEDICATION

I dedicate this book to the memory of my parents, Sam and Riferle Randle-Jackson, and, especially to the memory of David and Bessie Jackson, who stepped up and became my mother and father, raised me in the fear and love of the Lord, and gave me daily life lessons, without which I would be just another Black statistic. To God be the Glory!

CONTENTS

FOREWORD

A quiet demeanor. A humble spirit. An unwavering faith in his Lord and Savior. A selfless caring for those less fortunate. A heart for missions. A love for and sense of pride in his family. These are just a few of the characteristics of Jim Jackson that I have come to appreciate during the fifteen years that I have known him and served with him on the Advisory Board of The Amy Foundation.

Jim is a gentle giant. When you first meet him, you are mesmerized by his stories of mission trips, his encounters, his knowledge, and his profound understanding of biblical teachings. He is a listener, taking the time to hear the needs of others. He is a doer, putting the needs of others before his own and acting on those needs.

But behind his keyboard, "the power of the pen" takes over, and this quite unassuming man becomes an impassioned and eloquent writer, teaching and preaching from his own personal experience. Jim's columns explain, enlighten, and inform. On subjects ranging from cultural disobedience, activist judges, and marriage to the true meaning of holidays, Jim's columns hit the mark. Put simply, "He gets it!"

He's not always serious, though. Jim can laugh at himself, and you will find yourself laughing with him as he tells the stories of his visits to the dentist, his plumbing catastrophes, and others.

While reading Jim's columns, you will laugh, learn, and be enlightened if you take his message to heart. And you will become a better person, a more patriotic American, a stronger Christian.

As Jim said in his acknowledgment at the beginning of this book, "To God be the Glory." Might I add, the thanks go to God from all of us for Jim Jackson, and for his willingness to share through his columns his Christian perspective on events affecting our world every day.

JAMES RUSSELL, JR. CEO
The Amy Foundation

RECAPTURING OUR CULTURE

Alexis de Tocqueville was amazed that America's power and success were as directly related to our faith as to our form of government, operated by, for, and of the people.

His homeland, France, was ruled by aristocrats, and the people had no say in governance. He also noted, in the midst of praising America, that a tyrannical nation can govern without faith but a just nation cannot. He would be shocked to view our nation in the twenty-first century. Our culture has been kidnapped. A major reason is that parents, as a whole, seem to have given up on their God-given responsibility to direct, train, and properly rear their children.

Every day, we hear stories about young children killing each other, husbands and wives murdering each other, children abducted from their homes and killed, etc. Public schools are armed camps in which offensive behavior by students against other students and teachers is the norm. Many offenders are given a pass, or the victim is blamed.

Greed has engrained itself in our society, and class warfare has created an atmosphere in which enormous awards are handed out by juries who believe that by doing so, they are striking out against "Big ___" (fill in the blank: oil, business, medicine, pharmaceuticals, etc.). We have reared our children to believe that they are owed the very best that life has to offer, without building a strong work ethic or striving for academic excellence.

Our children are blindly following a whole slew of dangerous "Pied Pipers," such as rap music and degenerate television programs that have pushed the envelope until it has fallen off the table; now they are pushing the table over the edge. Music videos glorify murder and rape. Thugs are presented as heroes, and the prison culture is rampant in society, from clothing styles to the dead end "attitude" so proudly displayed by many youngsters.

In a trance-like search for acceptance and relevance, parents applaud such degradation, choosing to try to befriend their young rather than make the effort to become responsible parents. Many parents not only allow their children to listen to such filth, they even join them.

Some parents justify this compromise by only allowing their kids to listen to "modified" versions of rap music, in which profane words are partially cut out, while leaving plenty of enunciation to discern exactly what the "artist" is saying.

Movie stars, who regularly violate moral standards of decency and honor in order to fulfill a role written by someone whose agenda includes the destruction of those principles and moral standards which contributed to the greatness of America. Shamefully, these people who obtain relevance by pretending to be someone they aren't, are honored regardless of what simplistic or anti-American drivel they spew.

At one time, all political arguments were couched in what was best for America. Today, a "gotcha" mentality in politics leads people to violate their own principles and even tell blatant lies in order to get the upper hand over their opponent.

We stand by as activist judges legislate from the bench, shredding the principles by which America was founded, and allowing and encouraging the propagation of almost any religion except Christianity. De Tocqueville also said, "America is great because America is good. If America ceases to be good, it will cease to be great." God, of course, said it best when He said, "Blessed is the nation whose God is the Lord."

If we are to continue to receive those blessings, parents and people of good will must take a stand, recapturing our culture by insisting upon honesty, decency, and adherence to Godly principles.

THE CURE FOR
"HOLIDAY DEPRESSION"

I read an article about "Holiday Depression," noting increased depression and sadness as Thanksgiving and Christmas approach. Not clinical depression, which often is exacerbated by the frenzied holidays, but the kind of deep unshakeable feelings of sadness and woe.

Many people become sad during this time of year because they lost a loved one around this same time of year, and, instead of happiness, the season brings despair. Still others become sad because they fail to grasp the true meaning of Christmas, and cannot conjure up many good things to be thankful about. Whatever the reasons for feeling sad during normally happy times, it is tough to get beyond it without help. When I experience sadness, unhappiness, I consider the plight of Horatio Spafford, born in Troy, New York, in 1828. Horatio grew up to become a successful lawyer with a wonderful family and a prosperous, happy life.

As he planned a family vacation to France and Switzerland, little did he know that he was about to experience despair and loss beyond his imagination. Just prior to their ship's departure, some last minute business prohibited him from traveling with his family. He planned to sail and meet up with them a few days later. Well into their voyage, a violent storm hit the ship, cutting it in two. All four of his daughters drowned. His wife, Anna, barely escaped death.

Despair and grief shrouded over him like a heavy blanket of woe as he read his wife's sad letter about the loss of all their children. He penned words to express both the despair that threatened to throw him into the deep hole it dug for him, and the indescribable hope and peace that comes from giving one's pain and grief to a loving Lord. In 2 Corinthians 4, we are told that for those who trust in Christ, "We are troubled on every side, yet not distressed; we are perplexed, but not in despair."

He wrote the hymn, "It is Well With My Soul," in which he describes sorrow "like sea billows" rolling over him. He also acknowledged that his sin, all of his sin, is nailed to the cross, and he writes about hope, in that the day will come when, "faith shall be sight, and the clouds be rolled back as a scroll…" He experienced severe grief and anxiety strong enough to overcome anyone, but he turned to the one who could give him the strength to withstand the pain by providing him with something to look forward to—the return of our Savior, and the knowledge that, in Christ, his soul is well regardless of the circumstances he may face.

Those who suffer from clinical depression often require professional treatment to deal with the symptoms. Placing one's burdens upon a living Christ can help even the most severe medical problems. Many who experience depression and sadness at Christmas may want to meditate upon the words of Horatio Spafford's moving and uplifting song.

It seems that people who are sad at Christmastime often

seem to focus upon their own needs and wants, like and dislikes. Instead of dwelling on themselves, they may find relief from their sadness in helping someone less fortunate, or by focusing on the many blessings they have rather than their losses and problems. The words of Horatio's song have, many times, lifted me beyond despair and given me hope. Because I have Christ as Savior and Lord of my life, I can rejoice in the holiday season and all seasons, and whatever plight I face, through Him, it is well with my soul.

WHY DOES GOD ALLOW
NATURAL DISASTERS?

I recently traveled to Sri Lanka to issue eye-glasses and help rebuild an orphanage that was destroyed in the devastating Tsunami wave that struck much of south Asia on December 26, 2005. More than 40,000 people were killed on this small island alone.

Many of the Sri Lankan fishermen lost their boats and nets, escaping with only their lives. Their homes were washed out to sea. Most of the women were seamstresses who lost all of their possessions, including eyeglasses, which are critical to their trade.

A fast-moving wall of water over forty feet high slammed the shore, and, just as quickly, receded, dragging people, homes and possessions back out to sea. It was breathtaking to witness the devastation it left in its wake.

One team member came upon a thin old man, standing alone on the seashore, arms outstretched, crying out to the vast Indian Ocean, "Why have you done this to me? Why did you destroy my family and my boat? Why? Why?"

Bill, the team member, photographed the forlorn man,

and later wrote a poem entitled, "Tsunami Man," in which he attempted to express the total sense of loss the man felt, and yet express how even Tsunami Man could have hope in the midst of pain.

Many Sri Lankans and people around the world ask, "Why?" Why does God allow disasters to destroy people and property? Is He angry with us? Does He simply hate us? Why does He allow children to die, and storms and earthquakes to come from nowhere, leaving such total destruction in their wake?

I didn't speak to the Tsunami Man, but I have spoken with others who asked the same questions, in Sri Lanka and around the world. The answer is always the same. God created the earth and the heavens, as well as all life. Mankind was His crowning glory of all creation since He created us in His own image.

The Bible tells us that we were meant to live forever, and death and destruction, deterioration and wasting away were not a part of the original plan. Mankind has brought all of the devastation upon ourselves through sin. The author of all sin, Satan, wreaks havoc upon the earth, mankind and everything in creation. God tells us that the wages of sin is death. The price for all sin required full payment. God knew that we could never pay the price, which is perfection, so He sent His son, Jesus Christ, to live a perfect life and to become the perfect, unblemished sacrifice—to pay the price for all sin. And He offers His free gift of eternal life to all who will receive it.

God tells us that we live only for a moment in this life, but our souls will live forever, either with Him in glory, or without Him, which He describes as hell. God will give those who believe in His Son new, indestructible bodies, and will create a new heaven and new earth; believers in Christ will abide with Him forever. That is the message Christ commanded us to bring to the Tsunami Man, and all who cross our path.

Whether we travel across the ocean or within our neighborhood, Christ asks us to reflect His love to all by our countenance, our willingness to help others unconditionally, and by letting others know that they do not have to live lives of despair. He even sends His powerful Spirit with us to give us the words to say and to prepare the hearts of others to hear His message of salvation.

With God doing all of the work, our tiny sacrifice of just making ourselves available isn't very hard to do. Is it?

AN "UNENLIGHTENED"
VIEW OF THE
CREATION/EVOLUTION FLAP

The origin of the earth has always been a mystery. Many who consider themselves enlightened believe that Creationism is improbable, even impossible, while accepting evolution and other theories as fact, with no tangible proof or rationale to substantiate the theory.

The thought of a Creator, somewhere out in the heavens, judging people and holding them to His standards is daunting, and makes our rebellious human nature uncomfortable. We'd rather believe humans are no different than animals or bacteria, and therefore, not accountable for their thoughts and actions. If we are here by accident and return to nothing when we die, then we can live as we please. And, one day man thinks he will even solve that death thing.

Evolution is taught as fact, even though it fails on many fronts. Still, science continues to research other possible answers to our origin. The scientific community will accept almost any theory other than the presence of an all-knowing Creator.

JAMES J. JACKSON

Polls show that fifty-eight percent of us believe that a divine intelligent designer created us. Seventeen percent believe that life was created when a comet struck the earth. An equal number believe all life crawled out of an ancient lake, and the remaining respondents believe aliens from outer space brought life to earth.

There is also "The Big Bang" theory, in which everything was created at once by a loud bang! One Christian writer wrote that this may be the closest theory to reality, opining that God spoke, and *Bang!*, all creation came into existence. The obvious response to Evolutionists is, "Who created the ancient lake, or the aliens, and the comet?" Each theory raises more questions than answers.

There are scientific explanations for the changing seasons; the earth, moon and sun moving in their paths; bird and animal migrations, etc., but those explanation prove, rather than disprove creation. If all things were caused by mistake, or randomly, why then doesn't the sun rise in a different area of the sky each morning, and why do seasons come in order? And why are the phases of the moon predictable? Why not eight phases one month, and two the next month?

The Bible tells us that God created everything, but that He created mankind in His own image, with special attributes, such as the ability to reason, to solve problems and to build relationships, and communicate verbally.

Most of all, He gave us the ability to discern between right and wrong. Animals operate from instinct, a genetic code, which makes all animals within one animal family operate exactly the same. They cannot use reason or escape genetic limits. Although they can be taught tricks and the semblance of reasoning, it is only through a repetitive training process.

It may be that God, in creating the Universe, deliberately left many questions unanswered. Perhaps He endowed us with inquisitive minds, to hold our interest, and spark a quest to know Him more deeply. For centuries, people worshipped the moon, believing that the man in the moon watched over us.

Mankind figured out that the moon had a distinct effect upon ocean tides and other atmospheric conditions, but we are not able to determine exactly how it does. Many thought that the moon was made of green cheese. When we landed on the moon, we found absolutely nothing to explain the moon's effect on the earth, and, of course, no cheese. Perhaps God left such things unanswered in order to increase our faith in Him.

I would rather depend upon fact than theory. Our origin is clearly stated in the Bible, "In the Beginning, God created the heavens and the earth." By faith, we can believe and trust in that statement. Without faith, we will continue to wander in the wilderness of enlightened ignorance.

ACTIVIST JUDGES, POLITICIANS CAUSE MARRIAGE AMENDMENT

President Bush supports a Constitutional Amendment to protect marriage as the union of one man and one woman. How radical!

Many Americans agree that this step is necessary to stop activist judgers and elected officials from ignoring or outright disobeying current laws by "marrying" same gender people. There is, however, a different take on this that should be considered.

Some amendment opponents call it an unnecessary, lengthy process to challenge something that should be left up to each state. That argument fails in the face of a movement already afoot to force every state to honor "unions" condoned by other states.

Marriage was instituted by God for one man and one woman to enter into a lifelong covenant with God. God clearly does condemn gay unions, and even destroyed the cities of Sodom and Gomorrah because of homosexual activity, which is where the term "sodomy" originated. It was not intended for two men or two women to marry each other any more than for a person who deems himself "bisexual" to marry two people, one of each gender, or any other variation of "marriage."

Throughout the Bible, homosexuality is clearly condemned. The book of Romans clearly lays out the dangers of "men with men." Jesus himself said, "... Have you not read that he who made them from the beginning made them male and female ... and that the two shall become one ..." thereby instituting marriage as a holy union.

The proponents of gay marriage operate as though it has always been a fact of life that has now come under attack by "bigots," when the truth is that marriage between one man and one woman has always been the way society was ordered. How did our society arrive at this point? Changing the Constitution won't change the hearts and minds of people. Our culture has degraded so far that any prurient concept or activity may arise and flourish.

When AIDS began to devastate the homosexual community, society refused to admit that this type of behavior was spreading the disease. Now it is found in all segments of society.

When the North American Man-Boy Love Association appeared on the scene and was widely acceptable, we looked the other way. When gays labeled the Boy Scouts as bigots for refusing to allow gay scout leaders, we remained quiet.

The underlying causes of these problems are not legal in nature; therefore, a legal solution may not work. Like most current societal problems, these issues are spiritual and require a spiritual approach.

Christians have failed to bring the message of the Gospel to our people. People who do not know the love of Christ become their own gods. People who are ignorant of their sin condition and their need of a Savior assume that whatever they decide to do is inherently right. God says that there is a way that seems right to man, but that it ends in death.

More than eighty percent of Americans call themselves Christian, but we, by our silence, allow a tiny percentage of the population to dictate the moral direction of our nation. When we sit idly by and allow Christian, moral judicial candidates to be kept off the bench while judges with a proven track record of anti-Constitution and anti-God decisions are placed in critical positions, we fail society. When we do not hold politicians to God's standard of right and wrong, and cheer bad behavior, we neglect our responsibility to elect morally sound people, opening the door to anti-family and ungodly concepts.

Christians must take a stand to turn this nation around. If we don't repair the moral condition of our nation, a Constitutional amendment would be like rearranging the deck chairs on the Titanic.

PROTECTING FRAGILE YOUNG
MINDS AT HALLOWEEN

When someone writes about the dangers of Halloween, people are quick to shout, "It's only make believe. Let the kids have a little fun!" I have been accused of being a stick in the mud at times because I expressed dismay at costumes that appear satanic or those representing evil characters.

Halloween can be a harmless day of fun and make-believe. But, if handled in the wrong manner, it can send unclear signals to impressionable young minds, leading them to inadvertently worship, or at least give homage to, dangerous entities that many of us would rather avoid thinking about.

I don't call for the abolition of Halloween, but I do often ask parents to ponder what they are glorifying when they dress their little treat-seekers in costumes. I believe some of Satan's most effective deceptions are those in which evil and its effect upon us is minimized or even laughed at.

When our children were small they dressed up in costumes and attended programs at their school, where they had parades, played games, and enjoyed snacks. They also made posters and talked about Reformation Day, which also falls on October 31, the date on which Martin Luther nailed his list of theses to the church door to protest the church's departure from Holy Scripture. His actions launched the Reformation, which spawned the various Lutheran denominations.

Parents were encouraged to dress their children in costumes such as angels, knights, princes and princesses, patriots—any costume that did not conjure up evil notions or give glory to violence, evil, or satanic practices. From witnessing the glee experienced by the participants, I don't believe they missed any fun by the lack of such costumes.

The belief that ghosts, demons, witches and warlocks do not really exist is a dangerous deception that can cause one to ignore what the Bible tells us about such things. In Galatians 5, it lumps idolatry and sorcery with many other sins that prevent one from inheriting the Kingdom of God.

In Ephesians 6:12 we are warned that we are not in a battle between flesh and blood, but "against the rulers, against the authorities of the world of this darkness; against the powers of spiritual forces of evil in the heavens." I don't believe that this precludes us from allowing our children to have fun and enjoy the thrilling world of make-believe. Pretending is a very vital part of growing up, and should be encouraged.

Several places in the Bible speak about ghosts and spirits, such as when the disciples were frightened when they saw Jesus walking on the water. They feared he was a ghost. When Jesus appeared in the room after his resurrection, they thought he was a ghost, and were not convinced until he ate some bread and fish with them.

Every mention in the Bible of ghosts, demons, spirits, sorcery and such practices is laced with fear and evil, and is presented as something to fear and avoid rather than something to make light of or emulate. So it appears that Halloween can be celebrated by children, complete with wearing costumes, and it can be harmless if parents simply stop and think before buying costumes.

Parents should consider exactly what the costumes their children wear really represent. Does the costume give glory to those things that God says we should not glorify, or does it simply represent someone or something that really is harmless?

We must be careful that we don't inadvertently give our young children a lax attitude toward some entities and activities that we are warned against in Scripture. And that can be easily accomplished without taking the fun out of Halloween.

HONESTY AND HONOR FORGOTTEN IN IRAQ WAR PROTESTS

I t has become fairly clear that the Iraq War protestors, by and large, have a credibility problem. Their reasons do not line up with the truth. Honesty and honor are wounded in the process.

After the 9/11 attacks, the President promised that those responsible for carrying out, sponsoring, and supporting the attacks would be held accountable. He also warned any nation or group involved in terrorism that they would be stopped. This war is a major effort toward that goal.

Those who protest for "peace" probably would have had a greater impact on avoiding war had they protested Saddam Hussein's terrible human rights record, and encouraged him to give up his weapons. Instead, they have, arguably, emboldened Saddam by acting as though he is some kind of folk hero and victim. Many anti-American groups saw this as a chance to gain converts by sponsoring protests and marches.

Yes, protest (or as outlined in the Constitution, redressing our government) is our right. The problem is that many protestors are driven by a vicious hatred for President Bush personally, which keeps them from thinking clearly. High-profile Hollywood actors have been outspoken and full of vitriol in their protest. Several entertainers even spoke out against the United States on foreign land. Some of them have since complained that they have lost contracts, or that sales of their music or movies have fallen drastically.

These folks don't seem to realize that their right to free speech doesn't include a guaranteed soap box from which to spew their hatred for their country and its leaders. No, that soapbox was paid for by people who appreciated the talent these people displayed, but never asked for their political views.

The recent Academy Awards program, which usually commands enormous attention from viewers, experienced the worst ratings in memory. Why? Many viewers who wanted to see who won awards refused to subject themselves to immature, inaccurate ravings from people whose anti-American bent is no secret.

Perhaps the intellectual dishonesty from so many high-profile protestors is turning the tide against them. Most protestors declare that this war is immoral and will take many innocent lives. They don't find it immoral, however, to take the life of an unborn or "partially born" child, although God clearly warns against harming children.

They also do not consider it immoral to make movies and videos with blasphemous themes that glorify anything dishonorable or decadent. Nor do they consider it immoral or wrong to jump from spouse to spouse, or to live together unmarried. They opine that their lifestyles are their business, but when one opens the door with declarations of what is wrong or immoral, it exposes their hypocrisy.

Many groups "protest" through various depraved activities, including stripping off their clothes, vomiting in public, and other equally appalling ways of calling for the downfall of America. We have a guidebook that outlines what is truly moral and immoral, right and wrong: the Bible.

Also, people who want presidents and government officials to govern based upon polling results ignore polls when the results don't fit their agenda. Polls show that nearly seventy percent of Americans believe it was right to liberate the Iraqi people, yet the protestors apparently believe the thirty percent who oppose should sway the president's decisions.

And those who believe that there is never a reason for war should read the book of Ecclesiastes chapter 3, which states that "there is … a time for birth, a time for death … a time for killing, a time for healing … a time for tearing down and a time for building," etc. As long as humans exist, there will be reasons for war. Fighting for freedom and justice is an honorable reason.

IN OUR OWN IMAGE

Author David Voltaire said, "God created man in His own image; and man has been returning the favor ever since." Never has this been truer than it is today, when people increasingly invoke the name of Jesus to justify actions that more likely stem from their own sinful nature than from divine inspiration.

When the "What Would Jesus Do?" fad began, young people wore the slogan on bracelets, t-shirts, etc. But before long, it was quite obvious that many of them simply claimed that whatever they decided to do was exactly what Jesus would do under the same circumstances.

A teenager was admonished for embarrassing a young girl by loudly bringing attention to a very visible birthmark on her face. The teen stated that Jesus said that the truth will make you free, and he had only spoken the truth. Of course, he wasn't truly trying to be like Jesus, but rather was using Jesus as an excuse to hurt another person. What Jesus actually taught us is that if we abide in him, we will know the truth, and the truth will make us free.

When we claim to follow Jesus and then deliberately say or do something that is out of Jesus' character as clearly outlined in Scripture, we are recreating Jesus to be like us, not molding ourselves around his nature.

Even our Supreme Court is not immune to this trend. Its building is adorned with the Ten Commandments, and each session is opened with prayer, asking for the Lord's guidance. Then, with that formality out of the way, they proceed to take such steps as banning the Commandments from schools, courtrooms and other public places.

Our beloved and revered Bill of Rights states that our rights emanate from our Creator, but according to polls, many Americans believe that same Creator endowed us with the right to kill unborn children. No, I believe it is our desire to have a way around the consequences of wrong behavior or our need to not be inconvenienced that has led us to buy the lie that we have a God-given right to "choice."

Many people say that we should love unconditionally, as Jesus does, but what they mean is that we should overlook sin and wrong. That is not the way Jesus loves. He wants us to be distressed by our sin and to confess and repent to Him; then He forgives us. God loves us, but prescribes certain punishments for unrepentance. Everyone Jesus forgave, He told to go and sin no more. Man encourages others to continue in their sin with no fear of punishment because God loves them.

Recently, a leader in the Episcopal Church, during an interview about that church's recent appointment of an openly homosexual man to the level of bishop, said that Jesus never specifically said that homosexual activity was wrong. He dismissed biblical passages that were suggested as either being from the Old Testament and therefore irrelevant, or from the New Testament but not spoken directly by Christ. The interviewer didn't go further, but if this church leader truly believes that the entire Bible is the inspired Word of God and that Jesus is the only Son of God, then Jesus is also the author of everything in the entire Bible.

God warns those who do not hold to the truth of Scripture that on the day when they call, "Lord, Lord," He will say, "Away from me, I never knew you!" We must be careful to hold strictly to God's Word, and avoid what Pastor Herbert Geisler once called, "putting words in God's mouth."

DEATH BY A THOUSAND CUTS?

The alarming increase in violence by kids, character lapses, increased drug use, and other social problems have launched a multitude of "experts," each of whom believes he has the answer to our problems. They blame parenting, weapons, spanking, or bad toilet training. Many experts say we are all to blame. It is impossible to blame any one catalyst for all of our social problems. No one element has caused the muddy slide of our nation into the pigpen of decadence. No one issue or concept is threatening our existence as a nation, but perhaps we are dying a "death by one thousand cuts."

Aside from the fact that pure evil can manifest itself even in the minds of children, is society really liable for the increasingly vile actions of our citizens, old and young? Or are such nefarious deeds merely further evidence of a nation that has lost its moral compass? While no single ethical slip is enough to destroy our nation, hemorrhaging from so many moral "cuts" could very well cause us to bleed to death and possibly cease to exist as a republic. Let's consider some of the "cuts" threatening our downfall.

We allowed atheists and anti-Christians to prohibit prayer, or even Bible reading in schools and public places, while allowing (even encouraging) the teaching of pagan beliefs and concepts to our young. The U.S. Supreme Court, sitting in a chamber adorned with the Ten Commandments, opined that the Founders intended to prohibit prayer in public places.

We devalue the unborn by labeling them mere masses of tissue with no rights until birth, but God says, "Before I formed you in the womb, I knew you; Before you were born I sanctified you..." (Jer. 1:5). After sacrificing millions of "fetuses" on the altar of self, convenience, and "choice," it is now legal to kill a living baby, leaving the head in the womb to relegate the child to the legally expendable "unborn fetus" classification.

We readily accept concepts in child rearing that reject God's way. The Bible says not to spare the rod. Experts say spanking a child teaches violence, and as a result, children are running rampant in schools, homes and on the streets. We each have an inbred need for boundaries. Experts call violent activity a cry for help, but it is more often a cry for boundaries. As one movie line goes, "Somebody *stop* me!" Experts and so-called child advocates have suppressed any notion of God in kids' lives, so we can't convince the child that actions are wrong based upon God's law, and labeling activity as wrong based upon the view of parents, teachers, etc, falls upon deaf ears. The child knows how fallible adults are. We try to instill self-esteem without self control or self-respect, which is futile.

We accept such concepts as secular humanism and "situational ethics" (nothing is absolutely right or wrong; each person decides what is right or good for himself). We praise the lack of character while ridiculing anyone who pleads for a stronger moral focus. We allow people to feed self-destructive concepts, such as hip-hop and rap music, to our children. The Bible tells us of doomed societies in which, "... everyone did what was right in his own eyes."

Charlton Heston once said that our country's fabric is being torn apart, leaving us like a nation of warring gypsy camps, each with its own agenda, and no moral compass. Many would agree that we have fallen away from God's rules and standards for living and for rearing children and ordering society, to our detriment.

We don't need more human "experts" to bring us humanistic explanations and cures. We, as a nation, must turn back to the only real "Expert," and follow His "Operating Manual" for living.

MEMORIAL DAY: A DAY OF PROFOUND MEMORIES

Memorial Day began as Decoration Day in 1868, when Union soldiers and sailors chose May 30 as a day to decorate the graves of soldiers who died in the Civil War. In 1971, Congress declared the last Monday in May as the federal holiday, Memorial Day, to honor those who died in military service to the United States.

It appears that relatively few of the young people today have any idea of what Memorial Day represents. This may indicate another area in which we, as a society, have neglected to give our youth a well-grounded understanding of the many concepts and belief systems that contributed to America becoming a great nation.

It is more politically correct to honor movie stars and thugs and gangsters than those who risk all in the name of freedom. It appears that, sadly, love of country is not taught as in the past. Many people seem to show disdain for those who believe that our way of life is worth fighting for. A strong sense of loyalty doesn't come through osmosis. It is taught, as it was taught to me.

Memorial Day holds profound memories for me. My family often spent the holiday visiting cemeteries. My parents had both died before I was five, so my aunt and uncle, my adoptive parents, always took us to visit the graves of my parents and other deceased family members.

We visited the graves of relatives who had died either in World War II or the Korean conflict. On the way, we stopped to pick up Cousin Larry at Hines, Illinois, a Veteran's hospital so large that it had its own postal zip code.

Larry lost both legs in Korea and lived at Hines hospital. In the 1950s there were few agencies to assist severely disabled persons, so he earned money making small trinkets to sell in the hospital's gift shop. He was a big, gregarious guy whose cheerful demeanor made others forget about his plight.

I remember wheeling Larry around the cemetery and watching his tears flow when we stopped at the graves of fellow Korean conflict soldiers. I witnessed the patriotism that flowed from Larry and my Uncle David, who had served as a Master Sgt. in World War II. He also served as a bodyguard for Joe Louis, the famous prizefighter. Since Louis was restricted from defending himself (his hands were considered "lethal weapons"), a capable soldier was assigned to keep others from "taking on the champ" for notoriety.

I will never forget the sight of a six-foot, four-inch truck driver and his wheelchair-bound nephew tearfully saluting before leaving the military section of the cemetery, with white crosses and Stars of David decorating graves. I remember returning to Hines and visiting with sick soldiers, some of whom had been in the hospital for many years and many who rarely, if ever, had any visitors.

I listened to many war stories, but, mostly, I learned

that these veterans loved their country, and would sacrifice more, if necessary, for our freedom. Most of them considered themselves fortunate, mourning those who gave the final measure.

We must remind our youth that many foreigners risk their lives to experience freedom in America, and that freedom is worth fighting for. We must teach them to honor those who serve to keep us free, and to love the only country most of them will ever know. We must teach them to honor those who loved America enough to give their lives for her. Jesus said that there is no greater love than when one gives his or her life for others.

LOOKING FORWARD TO
MY PERMANENT TEETH

When I talk about my extreme fear of going to the dentist, people often smile knowingly and offer that they, too, dislike having dental work done. But they really don't understand that when I say I fear dentistry, I mean dread, horror, and trepidation.

I was so traumatized as a child by what I remember as a sadistic dentist who loved to hurt children, that I avoided going for several years. I brushed and flossed extra diligently to make up for my absence in the "torture chair." I finally sought out a dentist after my wisdom teeth became so impacted that I couldn't stand the pain.

The dentist lectured me for my truancy, but was impressed that my teeth were in good condition in spite of the long gap in visits. Still, he saw enough work in there to assure his next month-long, spare-no-expense trip to the South of France. He began whimsically chattering about building bridges and tunnels and grinding teeth to even up my bite, etc. I thought I was about to die.

Well, I survived that visit by encouraging him to simply

(?) pull the wisdom teeth and send me on my way. From then on, the shrill, whinny sound of dentistry tools have been my "boogey man." A couple of years later, when I finally found the courage to return for a checkup and cleaning, I gravely, but in all sincerity, requested general anesthesia. He said "No" for the procedure. With every ounce of my strength, I gripped the ends of the dental chair armrests. I was so stressed that I went straight home and took a nap.

During the cleaning, the dreaded sound of an air tool filled the air, and soaked me in horror. I thought I felt excruciating pain, and told the hygienist so, to which she responded, "You can't be in pain. I am only polishing your teeth." I felt pain. That's my story, and I'm sticking to it.

For the past few years, I have dutifully gone in for my six-month check ups. The cleaning process still causes me pain, and, yes, I still sometimes take a nap afterward to let the blood return to my palms and fingers.

My daughters have obviously told my grandchildren the legend of my dental visits. I recently got a call from six-year-old Charlotte, who proudly advised me that she had gotten two fillings, and she was not going to take a nap.

I have also summoned up the courage to allow the dentist to perform some cosmetic and, according to him, critical dental work, including fillings, caps, and, even the dreaded root canal (a process no doubt created by Hitler's top torture experts). He still won't give me a general, and he thinks I enjoy laughing gas a little too much.

I recently was told that I was in desperate need of a crown, which the dentist decided to have made with an appliance by which to attach future bridgework. The slight alteration to the crown sent my insurer into orbit, requiring special approval. I finally had the crown installed. It was painful, but not as painful as the co-pay I was slapped with for a "non-standard appliance."

Dentistry is but another of life's challenges that those who trust in Jesus Christ for salvation won't have to face in Heaven. And because He became one of us, lived a perfect life and offered His life for mine, I won't suffer pain or fear for eternity.

Awaiting me are "permanent teeth," and a crown that is paid for because He lives.

A "GOOD AND FAITHFUL SERVANT" IS WELCOMED HOME

There is an explosion of biographies, autobiographies, and hit pieces written by or about public figures today. A rock star in her 20s just announced that she is writing her "memoirs." At such a young age, it's hard to believe she has enough material to fill a pamphlet, much less a book.

Ego and self-aggrandizement seem to be the driving force behind many of these books in today's "it's all about me" mindset. I would rather focus on people who, while they may never be the subject of a book, display nearly zero ego, and have a profound impact on countless people in ways that really matter.

One such person was Phil Lee, who had a rare love for others. He was not driven by self-satisfaction or personal gain, but he had a heart to share in a gift he had received. He wasn't a loud or boisterous person, but one who preferred to speak quietly and one on one.

Phil was as at ease in a boardroom or before a group as he was on his beloved motorcycle. At all times, the foremost thought in his mind was finding the one person with whom he was supposed to talk at that time and place. Like the old TV show, *The Millionaire*, Phil had an assignment. But he shared a gift that was worth much more than a million dollars.

Phil possessed the precious gift of eternal life offered freely by Jesus Christ through His death and resurrection. He had absolutely no doubt that eternity with Jesus awaited him one day, but Phil also knew that he had been commissioned by headquarters to pass on the gift.

While many Christians know they should go into the world and baptize people, many neglect the all important final part of their orders, which is disciple-making: teaching people to obey everything Christ taught us. Phil took this to heart, knowing that without being discipled (or taught) people risk missing out on the blessings derived from a deep and personal relationship with the Lord.

He knew that to become an effective tool in God's kingdom, he must first disciple himself—to delve into God's word for strength, wisdom, and knowledge. He realized the importance of identifying, confessing, and abandoning subtle and obvious sins that get in the way of a true relationship with Christ. He knew that this lifelong process was essential before attempting to disciple others.

Phil tuned his heart and mind into God's wavelength by always being open to spiritual promptings and never shying away from an opportunity to share his faith and then follow through by working with people to help them grow in their faith.

Phil gave his time and talents to Bible study, praying, and worshipping with all who crossed his path. He was not overbearing or forceful; just confident in his own relationship with the Lord, and patient and kind in helping others develop a like relationship.

When Phil was diagnosed with terminal cancer, he didn't host a "pity party," but increased his efforts to disciple as many people as he could in the time he had left on earth. Scott Merritt, a businessman whom Phil mentored into a discipled life, says that he believes that God sent Phil to save his business and to turn his life around. He was most impressed by Phil's dedication to the work. When Phil was in his last days and could hardly function, he was heard to say, perhaps he could disciple just one more…

Phil knew the value of the gift of eternal life, and he answered the call to share it with everyone God brought across his path. He now rejoices in Heaven, and we who knew him rejoice in the memory of his dedication to the task that Jesus gave to all of us. He undoubtedly has heard his Lord's words, "Well done, good and faithful servant; enter into the joy of your Lord." It is my prayer that others will follow Phil's example and take to heart the work that our Lord assigned us.

PLUMBING: A GREAT SOURCE OF HUMILITY

In *Dirty Harry*, Clint Eastwood declared, "A man's got to know his limitations." True statement. When we refuse to acknowledge our limitations, disaster often results.

I'm fairly handy around the house, but when it comes to plumbing, my disasters are legendary. Every plumbing job from changing an aerator to a installing a toilet seat has become a catastrophe, so one would think that I would have learned my limitations.

Not so. Whenever my family sees me with a plumbing tool, they all but tackle me to stop me. They have good reason for their trepidation. My most memorable plumbing calamity began as a simple toilet stool seat replacement. Simply unscrew the two plastic nuts underneath the bowl rim. But they were corroded and wouldn't budge, so I tried to use a screwdriver and my "all-purpose tool," the hammer, to loosen it.

As I struck the screwdriver, it slipped, punching a one-inch hole in the bottom of the bowl. In a quick out-of-the-mind experience, I decided to flush the toilet. My wife knew that my latest plumbing disaster had begun when a large water stain crept across the ceiling directly below me. It's amazing how quickly a couple of gallons of water can become a little pond from such a small hole. By the time I cleaned up the water, the stores were closed. I placed an "out of order" sign on the toilet. The next day I began checking the cost of a replacement toilet.

The plumbing shop required the exchange of the old toilet. This took quite some time, since I had to remove the floor bolts and disconnect the tank. I suppose I should have tried to dip the water out, but you guessed it, I flushed it again. I managed to catch most of the water, but not all of it. I took the toilet and exchanged it and headed home.

My confidence soared as I skillfully installed a new "wax ring," secured the toilet to the floor, and victoriously attached the new seat, which had started the whole thing. My victory bubble quickly burst when I found that the holes in the new toilet didn't line up with those in the old tank!

I called the plumbing shop, and was told to bring in either the toilet or the tank to match up with the right component. The inside of the tank consisted of so many moving parts, I opted to return the toilet. So, on day three I installed the new toilet. My neighbor, whose wife calls him "Tony, the Toolman," came over to help me.

We attached the tank to the toilet. Then I went to answer the phone while Tony secured the floor bolts. I heard him yell what must have been a German expletive. "You didn't!" I yelled. "I did!" he yelled. He had tightened one side down too far, and when he tightened the other bolt, the toilet base broke in half.

The guy at the plumbing shop laughed much louder and longer than necessary before agreeing to replace the toilet for free. But, while dumping the water into the tub, it slipped and broke a large porcelain soap dish.

On day four I exchanged the toilet and installed it without further trauma, but every time it is flushed it makes a rumbling, burbling sound. Whenever I reach for my tools to fix it, my family insists they don't hear anything, and my wife points to Ecclesiastes 3 ("…a time to love; hate; heal; etc."), and reminds me that it does not mention a time to do plumbing. I am learning my limitations.

RIGHTS, RESPONSIBILITY, AND SACRIFICE

Freedom isn't free. That's my message to athlete Toni Smith, who turns away from the U.S. flag during the national anthem to protest "inequities imbedded in the American system."

She also says, without substantiation, that America has killed "millions of innocents." She has been jeered and told to leave the country. A Vietnam veteran tried to force her to look at the American flag. Her supporters cite her Constitutional right to free speech and expression, declaring that many people fought and died for her right to desecrate or disrespect the flag. I agree that she has a right to protest, but our rights are multifaceted. They come with responsibility and sacrifice.

We have a responsibility to those who bought our freedoms with their lives to be honest and to be grateful for what they did. Americans who died to establish and to defend this nation did so to protect our rights, assuming that the beneficiaries of their sacrifice would honor and cherish their efforts.

No soldier goes to war believing that Americans would

squander their rights by desecrating the flag, or calling for America's downfall. Most soldiers who died in battle, like the founders who risked all for our life, liberty, and pursuit of happiness and the right to speak freely, more likely assumed that their actions would be honored by the recipients of freedom.

Many of those who evoke the First Amendment often pick and choose whose rights they will defend. Smith's defenders believe a student has a right to shun or burn the flag, but has no right to pray or even speak of God in a public assembly.

Toni Smith quotes an old 60's mantra, "It will be a great day when schools have all the money they need, and the military has to hold bake sales to buy bombs," which, coupled with her inaccurate "slaughter of innocence" assertion, shows that her position stems more from the philosophy of the "blame America first" crowd than from her own convictions.

History proves that America strives to be honorable and humanitarian. When we attacked the Taliban, who murdered women for teaching girls to read in Afghanistan, and who led the 9/11 attack, we air-dropped food to the citizens. We give foreign aid to those sworn to destroy us.

The Constitution does not give us the right to call for the destruction of the U.S., which many of the current anti-war protestors are doing. A young friend was shocked at a recent march in Washington, D.C., when he heard several speakers call for the annihilation of America. He was angry that he and others had been duped to beef up the numbers at a rally sponsored by organizations such as the American Communist Party and other seditionist organizations.

No, Toni Smith, Americans did not give their lives in

the hopes that you would dishonor the flag for which they fought. They risked their lives and often made the ultimate sacrifice because they believe in our representative form of government, which is the envy of the world. They did and do so in hopes that others will understand that America, with all her faults, is worth fighting and dying for.

It doesn't take much sacrifice to dishonor the flag, but Jesus described those who have died to give you that right when He stated "there is no greater love than to give one's life for others." Then He proved it in a most astounding way. Ms. Smith has a right to protest, along with a responsibility to be honest. I just pray that it doesn't take the loss of freedom to show her how precious it is.

A PERMANENT SOLUTION TO A TEMPORARY PROBLEM

Most of us have experienced the gut-wrenching sadness and despair that comes with the news that a loved one or friend has committed suicide. I have experienced this several times during my lifetime, and it never becomes easier to understand or endure.

When I was about ten years old, our next-door neighbor, Mr. Terrell, overcome with grief from the death of his beloved wife, locked himself in his garage, started his car, lay down beside the exhaust pipe, and asphyxiated himself. Since he professed to be a Christian, the act bewildered and confused me. Even more confusing was the very terse discussion among the adults in my family about the state of Mr. Terrell's soul.

Years later, a close friend killed himself in a fit of desperation and hopelessness over mounting gambling debts and alcoholism. There was a great debate over where he would most likely spend eternity.

A few years later yet another friend committed suicide because he could not cope with his wife's death and the loneliness and failed attempts to replace the lost love and friend-ship they had shared for so many years. Both friends felt that their families would be better off without them.

They couldn't have been further from the truth. The first friend's family pretty much fell apart, each one blaming himself or herself for their father's death. The second friend has missed many, many precious moments, like births and achievements by his children and grandchildren. How sad.

I have spoken to ministers and theologians about suicide, and their opinions vary greatly. One minister felt that suicide dooms one to hell because it is "the only sin for which one cannot repent." Another believed that it is the ultimate act of rebellion against God, and therefore is unforgivable. Neither was unable to provide scriptural evidence of their position.

Recently, during a discussion about suicide, one friend asked me, "I know you're not a minister, but you are a mis-sionary, and I know you read the Bible regularly; so, what do you think about suicide?" First, I affirmed that I would never consider taking my own life because I am too curious about what tomorrow may bring, and I am too realistic about the effect upon my family and friends.

Then, I expressed that I had learned in evangelism train-ing that the Bible says, "The wages of sin is death, but the gift of God is eternal life …" I also learned that one sin is not greater than another or more punishable than another. God looks upon all sin as worthy of the "eternal death" penalty.

I also learned that we humans forget a great majority of thoughts, words, and deeds that we think, say, and do. If one bad thought can condemn me, then something that I forgot, and thereby failed to specifically repent of would be unfor-given and I would be doomed.

Our salvation is not determined by what we do, but by

what Jesus Christ has already done: paid the price for all of our sins. When we receive Him as Savior and Lord, and accept the free gift of eternal life, as John 3:16 tells us, we receive the unmerited free gift. This doesn't give one license to commit suicide or any other sin, and whether a person who commits suicide is allowed into Heaven is wholly in the Lord's hands.

One statement sums it up nicely: "Suicide is a permanent solution to a temporary problem." A better plan is to place our complete trust in our Creator, and turn our burdens over to Him.

THE BLESSING OF
TAKING A STAND

I f all of your friends jumped over a cliff, would you do the same?" Parents have posed this question to their children for generations, usually after a child asserts that "everyone else" is allowed to participate in some activity that is off-limits to him.

The obvious answer is, "No." Or, it used to be. Today, it seems that many people of all ages seem to operate in a pack mentality, whereby the one with the most influence is more often than not the most dysfunctional of the group. Almost daily we hear of people of weak character being led into crime, drugs, and self-destructive activity.

Gang activity is at an all-time high across the nation. Kids join and follow whoever is the dominant personality. Many people in prison are there because they blindly followed another person or group into criminal activity rather than taking a stand. The concept of standing alone on principle seems to be lost.

"Mike," recently honorably discharged from the Army, became friends with a group of young men with whom he had little in common other than a love of rap music. After several weeks of hanging out with his newfound friends, Mike began taking on their characteristics. He was unmotivated, began using marijuana, and slid toward trouble. One day, while the group was sitting around, someone suggested that they rob a bank. Mike knew that this violated every principle he had been taught but didn't have the nerve to stand up to his friends.

Mike decided that if he took only a minor role, he could please his friends without really violating his values. He sat in the getaway car with the driver, but when they were all captured in the unsuccessful crime, he, too, was charged with bank robbery. Now Mike has plenty of time to consider the consequences of compromising his principles rather than standing alone.

Another young man I know personally, "Aaron," was a good student. He participated in class, did well on tests, his attendance was excellent; yet his teacher reported that he rarely turned in homework assignments. This perplexed his parents, because they monitored his homework, and knew he completed every assignment. When asked about this, Aaron explained that other black kids ridiculed him when he turned in homework assignments, accusing him of "acting white." His father assured Aaron that he should fear failure and the consequences of deliberately disobeying the rules more than the loss of his friends' approval. They began a regular Bible study based upon what God tells us about standing alone and clinging to biblical morality.

Young people have to be taught to stand alone, even where fads are concerned. My twelve-year-old grandson wanted to have his ear pierced because nearly every boy in his class wore an earring. I asked the significance of an earring, and he didn't know. When I asked him not to have his ear pierced, he expressed concern that others would think that he considered himself better than them. I explained to him that he should simply tell his friends that this may be something they desire for themselves, but that the men in our family do not pierce their ears.

The Bible includes many stories about people who took a stand on principle. Joshua, when everyone seemed to be moving away from God's laws, stated, "As for me and my household, we will serve the Lord." Psalms 1:1 tells us that one who refuses to be with sinners or the scornful, or to take the counsel of the ungodly will be blessed.

I'd rather take a stand on principle than suffer the consequences of following the crowd.

REMEMBER YOUR VALENTINE

Valentine's Day has become so commercialized that its true meaning is often distorted or totally missed. More than a billion Valentine's Day cards will be given, millions of flowers, gifts, and boxes of candy will be delivered, and the economy will be noticeably enhanced.

Many people simply see this day as a special day to tell someone how much they love him. Few people seem to know the origin of the giving of valentines or hearts to others. There are many versions of the story, but basically, it seems that a priest named Valentinus, or Valentine, and his family assisted Christian martyrs who were persecuted by the Roman Emperor, Claudius, in the third century a.d.

Claudius outlawed marriage because he believed married men made poor soldiers because of the emotional attachment to their families. Valentine encouraged young lovers to visit him in secret, where he performed the sacrament of matrimony. Claudius, upon hearing of this, had Valentine brought before him. He was impressed with Valentine's conviction and inner strength, he offered to spare him from execution if he would renounce Christianity and convert to the Roman gods. Valentine not only refused to renounce Christianity, but attempted to convert the emperor, and was sentenced to death.

He was thrown into a dungeon. A jailer named Asterius had a blind daughter who brought food to Valentine. They became friends and she delivered messages to his friends for him. His clandestine notes to his loved ones always ended with the phrase, "Remember your Valentine." The night he was executed, he wrote a farewell message to the girl, and signed it, "From your Valentine."

He was beaten and beheaded on February 14, 273 a.d., in Rome. In the fourth century, Pope Julius I built a church in honor of Valentine. Over the years, the Valentine has become the universal symbol of love, affection, and friendship.

Love has become one of the most misunderstood and misused institutions, causing indescribable pain on the one hand, while bringing immeasurable feelings of joy and happiness on the other. Love can be used to manipulate, control hurt, and destroy when it springs from improper motives. Love that is given with conditions and strings attached can become a noose around the neck of the recipient, while unconditional love can be a wonderful, fulfilling experience for both people involved.

Love is repeatedly explained and demonstrated throughout the Bible. God must have known how self-centered mankind can be, so He commanded us to "Love your neighbor as you love yourself." When asked who is our neighbor, Jesus explained that it is everyone with whom we come in contact.

There is the kind of love that a parent has for his or her children. This type of love is deep and longing. It is filled with anticipation and expectations, fears for their safety, and pride in their accomplishments. The Bible talks about how special the love between a man and woman can be. It is very special when the sight of your loved one delights your spirit, and his or her voice makes your heart leap, when a warm feeling fills you from head to toe when you meditate upon the person who completes you and makes you whole.

Jesus taught us how to love by loving so unconditionally, that He suffered and gave His life to pay for our sins—everyone's sins. Even the sins of those who hate Him. He offers Heaven as a free gift to all who accept it, repent of their sins and receive Him as Lord a of their lives. Sounds simple? That's true love.

WHOSE VALUES SHOULD
WE EMBRACE?

I t seems that nearly everyone is talking about values: family values, societal values, etc. Political correctness tells us that the concept of values is fluid, and differs from one person (or even one situation) to the next. In fact, they believe nothing is really right or wrong; nothing is absolute, but flows with and is determined by the present situation.

The dictionary definitions for values includes:

Values are principles. But, many people today believe that one can live life without principles, guided only by the whim of the day. Many people believe in "situational ethics" in which right and wrong are determined by the situation, or one's current "feelings," rather than by a set code of behavior.

Values are standards. But we are led to believe that no standards should exist, especially regarding morals and ethics. Each person is to be left to his or her own interpretation of good and bad, right or wrong.

Many politicians believe our values are measured by how well government can manage and fulfill the lives of the citizenry. Principles such as integrity, honesty, and honor are often set aside while politicians attempt to implement our values as seen through their perspective.

Some schools offer classes in "values clarification." Apparently, a person who is confused as to what his values are can learn to clarify exactly how he should feel and think about life.

The United States of America became the greatest, most prosperous nation in history through God's divine providence. We didn't get to that place amidst confusion as to what we believe, or due to the lack of standards or principles. Most of those who built this nation had a firm grip on their faith and knew what they believed.

America experienced its strongest growth and prosperity during the periods when strong principles and standards dictated the daily lives of the majority of its citizens. If such principles as love of God, country, and family had not been deeply ingrained in our hearts and minds, we would not have won the Civil War, which defeated slavery, or the World Wars, which freed much of the world from tyranny.

Our principles led us to rebuild the nations of our enemies, to drop food for the citizens of nations at the same time we bombed those who held them in bondage. It seems that each time America faces a war situation, many people express concern that we will conquer and occupy another nation. We have never done so, and never will, because it violates our basic values and principles.

Values include a set of principles and a code of conduct by which one orders his life, that anchor life. The company executives and politicians who have been caught accepting graft or stealing through deceptive accounting practices either have no core values, or chose to ignore them in for self-gratification.

Core values are not made up as we go along, or based upon the direction of the wind. They are outlined in the Ten Commandments, and do not change based upon shifting social norms. God tells us that we should not steal, kill, or covet what belongs to others. He wants us to adopt moral standards and core values and virtues like love for others, joy, peace, longsuffering, gentleness, goodness, and faith. Such attributes were once an integral part of the American fiber.

If we get back to the business of training our children based upon what God says is right and wrong and placing God's standards in their hearts, rather than following flawed human "feelings" to plot life's course, we will see a great improvement in our quality of life.

FINDING THE CAUSE
OF VIOLENCE

H ow can society stop violence?" The opinion page "Question of the Week" caught my eye, so I read the responses to see whether any of them held the answer to one of mankind's oldest questions.

Even when "society" consisted of only two adults and two children, violence reared its ugly head. Cain killed his brother, Abel, out of jealousy, malice, envy, and every other evil motive known to mankind. Certainly, his parents felt that they had failed as parents.

Perhaps Adam and Eve, like many of the respondents, blamed the weapon. The biblical story, in Genesis, simply states that Cain, "... attacked his brother and killed him ..." without specifying what weapon, if any, was used. Today, the first response would probably be to make new laws limiting access to weapons. Perhaps Cain used only his fists, which would surely be a cause for arms control. Or, maybe he blamed real negative role models.

The letters to the editor covered a wide range. One letter writer even blamed the increase in violence on a "culture of violence" created by our health system, opining that the lack health benefits can spawn violent acts. Somehow, I find it hard to believe that universal health care would end violence as we know it.

Another writer quoted Mother Teresa, "There will be no peace on earth until there is peace in the womb." Yet another expressed that violence is inevitable, and that the womb and the tomb are the only places we can escape it. Everything else in between is doomed to chaos and violence. That writer was as fatalistic as Mother Teresa was simplistic.

One writer stated that America is more violent than other nations, as if all other nations are models of civility. Those who believe this concept need to get out more often. Anyone with foreign travel experience can attest that violence exists in every country. The truth is that the propensity for violence, from simple antagonistic behavior to murder, exists within every human being across the globe. The Bible tells us that because we all inherited Adam's sinful nature, all evil is conjured up within the human heart.

So, if we are all capable of all-evil acts, why does one person give in to crime, drugs, and an overall antisocial demeanor, while another strives to live a chaste, honorable life? It comes down to choices, habits, and daily life decisions. Some people become violence-prone because they were never taught self-control. God tells us, in Proverbs 16:32, that, "He that is slow to anger is better than the mighty; and he that ruleth his spirit than he that taketh a city."

God did not create us as robots. We have free will to either follow His laws or do evil. Violence, hatred, and malice, as well as honesty, love, and goodness all begin as seeds in one's life. Each person chooses which character traits he will embrace, nourish, and fertilize. A daily choice to nurture goodness and right living will cause those attributes to grow in one's life. Repentance and asking God's Holy Spirit to come into your life and lead and guide you will help you turn away from all manner of evil, including violence.

The root of violence can be explained using "the throne of life" illustration. When I sit on the throne of my life, I make decisions from a failed human perspective. But when Christ sits on my life's throne, I strive to make decisions that please Him. The question about the root of violence can be resolved by determining who is sitting on the throne.

TAKING CHRIST OUT OF CHRISTMAS IS MISSION IMPOSSIBLE

I recently met a young South Korean man who had come to America as an evangelist. I have traveled to many countries as a missionary, but it never occurred to me that America would ever need someone to come to our spiritual rescue.

I may have glimpsed the future. America has become complacent, taking for granted the many blessings that have come through our Judeo-Christian roots. An old tale says that a frog, placed in a pot of cold water on a stove will simply adjust its body temperature as the heat is increased, until it allows itself to be boiled to death without jumping out of the pot.

We have watched quietly as special agenda groups have kidnapped the morals of America. Those who do speak out against ungodly elements are labeled "intolerant" or simply "out of step." By our silence we empower groups who are determined to remove any vestige of Christianity from our midst. And the temperature rises.

The Ten Commandments, under vicious attack, are

banned from schools and many other public places, as if these words of wisdom from God Himself are detrimental to society and something to be feared and shunned. There is a growing movement to delete the national motto, "In God We Trust," from our money and coinage. Few are willing to raise their voices in opposition, for fear of being branded, "fundamentalist," or a "far-right-wing Christian." And the temperature rises.

Vows and oaths have been rendered hollow as one person after another commits moral malfeasance and violates the public trust. Their promises to adhere to certain conduct and standards are empty and meaningless because they are detached from any moral anchor. And the temperature rises.

One of the most alarming examples of the anti-God methodology is the blatant attempt to remove Christ from Christmas. From banning manger scenes in the public square to disallowing Christmas plays in schools, to vigorously discouraging the use of the word "Christmas," the goal of extracting Christ from Christmas is clear. "Happy Holidays" is the politically correct greeting for this time of year rather than "Merry Christmas," which is considered exclusionary and inappropriate. And the temperature rises.

At the same time, we allow our youth to glorify crime, drugs, and self-destructive people. We stood silently as a court attempted to remove "Under God" from our Pledge of Allegiance on behalf of a child who loves the Lord, but whose father lied and used her to further his own atheistic agenda. And the temperature rises.

So, when yet another generation grows up not knowing that a loving God created them and set forth certain moral rules for life, and when they fall deeper into the belief system that allows each person to decide what is right and wrong for himself, we will have no one to blame but ourselves.

Removing the name of Christ from Christmas is a futile endeavor. Since "Holiday" is a derivative of "Holy Day," reverence is given inadvertently. And Christ came to save the world regardless of whether we accept His gift of love, and changing words does not change what He has already done. As we allow our children to grow up without a relationship with the Lord, the day may yet come when America becomes a prime mission field of masses in need of the Savior we rejected.

We must stop taking God's Grace for granted. Christ warns us in Matthew 21:43, "Therefore I tell you, the kingdom of God will be taken from you and given to a nation producing fruit." Shall we produce fruit, or be boiled to death?

"COMMON COURTESY" NOT COMMON, BUT CRUCIAL

A woman gave my young grandson a small toy, which he took without comment. I told him to thank the lady, but this usually compliant child refused to say the words. The woman insisted that I should not force the child to say "thank you."

I told him to either thank the lady or return the gift. He reluctantly thanked her; then I explained to him that being thankful and courteous is as much for his own well being as it is for the person being thanked. Recently I witnessed a mother struggling to get her child to apologize for hitting another child. The amount of resistance the child displayed was alarming.

It seems that what used to be considered common courtesy is not so common anymore. Courtesy has been replaced by selfishness and an uncaring attitude toward others. Television programs and movies glorify the in-your-face approach to others and the "all about me" attitude. Young people either have lost or never grasped the art of kindness and respect.

Children who are not taught to treat others as they would want to be treated grow up to contribute to the crowded "Anger Management" classes and, in extreme cases, the prison population. Society seems to preach that being courteous, thankful, or apologetic shows some kind of weakness, when, in fact, it shows strength and self-control.

When our four daughters were young, they often had sibling spats. If two sisters displayed anger toward one another, my wife would often make them apologize to each other, then hug each other until both smiled. It is heartwarming to watch them pass on to their children the lessons of being courteous and loving toward their siblings and others.

During the 1970s, one small phrase in the movie, *Love Story* ("Love … means never having to say you're sorry"), put many viewers on the course toward today's attitude of failing to take responsibility for one's actions. It seemed such a profound line. In truth, love means caring enough about someone whom you may have offended or hurt to say you're sorry and take steps to make it right. It means caring enough to be thankful to others.

Many of today's distressing social and moral problems stem from a loss of the type of personal and societal ethics that for many years kept in check the level of animosity we showed each other. The Bible tells us to love our neighbor as we love ourselves. Jesus declared that, after loving God with all of our heart, soul, mind, and strength, loving each other is the greatest Commandment.

When we exhibit love toward each other, it illustrates God's love for us. Knowing and seeing all, He knew that His prime creation had fallen into deadly sin, and could not save itself. Rather than watch us struggle and give in and be lost for all eternity, He became one of us, in the Person of Jesus

Christ, and took the punishment for our sin and died for us. He then rose from the dead to show us that, through Him, we will rise again also. Any person, no matter how much sin baggage he or she is carrying, who repents, or apologizes to God, asks Christ to come into his or her life and be their Savior, and thanks Him for the free gift of eternal life, already has eternal life according to God's Word.

When we are loving and courteous with each other, we reflect our relationship with Christ, and we show His love to others. All He asks is that we share that love with others, through our actions and words.

WELCOME TO THE FRAY, MR. COSBY

Actor/comedian Bill Cosby recently ran afoul of the NAACP by speaking out against the degradation of academic and social skills among black youth, trends that today's black leaders would just as soon ignore. Many black leaders encourage anti-social behavior, knowing that prohibits young blacks from excelling. When the inevitable failure manifests itself, these leaders blame racism, genetic remnants of slavery, etc., and demand lower standards to allow these "victims" to prosper.

Dr. Cosby apparently believed the leaders shared his concern about the language many young blacks use today and its destructive effect upon any chance at success. He is undoubtedly taken aback by the harsh criticism he has received for speaking out. Cosby was expected to be funny and witty. He wasn't expected to take up the chant of victimhood by blaming every social problem on racism, but he wasn't supposed to challenge the leadership by attacking a problem they would rather not solve (failure is a necessary element for these leaders to feel relevant). But he did, and a firestorm has resulted.

Mr. Cosby said that many parents, "...are not holding up their end of this deal..." by failing to urge their kids to speak English properly, or to strive to excel in academics. Cosby stated, "They're standing on the corner and they can't speak English. I can't even talk the way these people talk: 'Why you ain't,' 'Where you is'... And I blamed the kid until I heard the (parents) talk. Everybody knows it's important to speak English except these knuckleheads.... They are buying (their kids) $500 sneakers... And they won't spend $200 for 'Hooked on Phonics.' You can't be a doctor with that kind of crap coming out of your mouth."

The NAACP leaders who followed were described as "stone faced," as they quickly reminded the crowd that most people on welfare are not black, and that the problems Cosby addressed are not self-inflicted. Cosby inadvertently placed himself at odds with those who, for a variety of reasons, promote Ebonics as a language or an English dialect. Many black leaders celebrate this rambling use of slang terms, knowing that it is self-destructive to speak that way.

Oakland, California, schools support Ebonics, or "African American Vernacular English," as an authentic dialect and even believe it is "genetic." Charles Fillmore, Professor of Linguistics at U.C. Berkeley, believes black people are born with a predisposition to speaking incorrect English.

So-called Ebonics is devoid of rules or order, and those who "speak" it would fight any such rules with the same fervor that they fight against proper English. It is very strange that the people who support and encourage Ebonics never seem to use it themselves. Many of those who loudly protested the old "Amos and Andy" series because of stereotypical language are now celebrating such slang as a birthright.

What Bill Cosby has hit upon is one of many areas where our culture has been hijacked by losers, and those who are out of the mainstream by virtue of bad choices and decisions. Rap artists and prison inmates coin many of the words and phrases that now replace proper English. Ebonics is simply a lazy way to rebel against decency and order.

Many leaders want to reward lack of effort or achievement with the best that society has to offer. If one does not strive to excel, one should not expect to receive the prize. Proverbs 13:4 still holds true today, "The appetite of the lazy craves, and gets nothing, while the appetite of the diligent is richly supplied."

LIVING AT PEACE IN A WORLD OF FEAR AND WORRY

Several surveys have been conducted recently inquiring whether fear of terrorism forces us to change or abandon travel plans, or alter our lives. Many respond that their lives have been greatly changed by worry over future terrorist attacks.

Since the 9/11 attacks, air travel has been down. American tourism to foreign destinations has also been negatively affected. While we haven't reached the "Chicken Little" desperation of running around and screaming, "The sky is falling! The sky is falling!" many of us spend an inordinate amount of time worrying about terrorism.

Worrying is part of the human condition. Our nature leads us to worry and fear the worst most of the time. My grandson worried about traveling to the west coast with his father, fearing that the aircraft would be hijacked or would crash. I was able to allay his fears by convincing him that worrying was unnecessary.

I reminded him that, technically, the people who died in the World Trade Center and the Pentagon all died in a plane crash, although none of them boarded a plane that morning.

He went and enjoyed the trip. He returned to tell how brave he was, and that he even comforted an elderly woman who was afraid to board the plane on the return trip.

Just as with most negative emotions, worry can become out of control and can consume a person if one allows it to continue to grow unbridled. Many of the phobias, or intense, irrational fears that attack people, stem from fear and worry. Fear of and worry about open spaces can cause a victim of agoraphobia to retreat into one corner of one room.

Fear of heights can begin with worry about great heights, but can degrade to the point that the victim cannot stand at the top of a short flight of stairs or look into a basement. Fear and worry can take away all initiative and keep people from becoming all that they can be. They crush the spirit and the ingenuity that might lead a person to seek excellence.

A person once said that the phrase, "What if…" is one of the devil's most powerful tools, because it plants the seeds of doubt that grow into fear and worry. Worry causes a person to look inward for answers to concerns and problems. But such answers do not reside within our weak, ineffective human nature.

The Lord wants us to turn our fears and worries over to Him. The Bible says, "Do not worry about anything, but in everything by prayer and supplication with thanksgiving let your requests be made known to God." God takes our fears and worries and either resolves the source of them, or uses them to bring glory to Him. When we understand that we are weak and unable to protect ourselves, we show reverence for God.

Even when our fears and worries are very well founded, we are to lean on God and not on our understanding or power. The twenty-third Psalms, in part, states, powerfully,

"…Yea, though I walk through the valley of the shadow of death, I will fear no evil; For You are with me; Your rod and Your staff, they comfort me." Knowing that God is with us in every situation, no matter how dangerous, is a great comfort to those who truly believe that God controls every situation, and has our best interest at heart always.

He reminds us that, even unto death, He is with us always, and because He lives, death has no power over us. That kind of love conquers worry and fear every time.

TEACHING LIFE LESSONS

My brother, who was visiting from Canada, helped me mow my mother-in-law's lawn while she was away. We mowed the grass, trimmed the bushes, and edged the sidewalks. Everything looked fine, except for the grass and weeds strewn along the sidewalk.

I had no broom or rake, and the house was locked. Knowing we couldn't leave it that way, we simply picked up the debris by hand. As we left, I pondered out loud why the thought of leaving that job undone had bothered me so.

My brother, Mel, stated that he felt the same way, and that is was probably because of the old saying that our parents instilled in us as we grew up: "If a task is once begun, never leave it 'til it's done. Be the labor great or small, do it right, or not at all." This sparked a conversation about how our parents used nearly every situation as a "life lesson."

We agreed that parents of today rarely seem to use proverbs or old sayings to instill character in their kids, instead allowing peers, TV, to dictate the moral direction of their children. Our parents seemed to have a saying to fit every circumstance. Some were quotes from philosophers or famous people, such as Ben Franklin's, "A stitch in time saves nine," but more often the sayings came from the Bible.

Many people know that their children need life lessons, but have no idea of how to provide them. Providing a moral direction for your children, admonishing and teaching them those tenets that will hold them in good stead for life is defined as discipling them.

Jesus Christ commissioned us to disciple others by saying, "All authority in Heaven and on earth has been given to me. Therefore, go and make disciples of all nations, baptizing them in the name of the Father, and of the Son, and of the Holy Spirit, and teaching them to obey everything I have commanded you. And, surely I am with you always, to the very end of the age."

One such command is to train our children in the way they should go, with a promise that when they grow old, they won't depart from it. Yet, parents often let opportunities to teach life lessons slip by. When a parent fails to give a life lesson, it leaves the child vulnerable to the traps and snares that await him because he is unarmed with the tools he needs to combat evil.

For instance, when a child has a habit of lying, parents often make light of it or ignore it, instead of teaching the child to be truthful, first because God commands it, and secondly because the child would want others to be truthful to him.

Parents should teach their children that the main motivation for doing what is right is because it honors God and the parents, and also that it builds the integrity and strength of character they will need to confront every evil and stumbling block they will face in the future.

We parents are given only one chance to instill godly

character, good habits, and work ethic in our children. When we remind them of how God would have them live their lives, and place Scriptures upon their hearts, we start them off on solid footing.

When we don't disciple our youth through the development of a personal relationship with their Savior, we leave them vulnerable, and, when adversity arises, they have no idea whom to turn to for safety and protection. I am thankful that my parents understood this concept.

GOD'S WORD FRUSTRATES
POLITICAL CORRECTNESS

It must be very frustrating to remain a member of the political correctness crowd these days. The concept is little more than an oxymoron which has wheedled is way into the American lexicon. It must require the believer to place common sense on a shelf, take a huge daily dose of intellectual dishonesty, and surrender independent thinking to the cause.

While political for sure, there is little correct about it. The underlying theme seems to be that mankind has no right to exist, and that plants and animals are somehow superior to us. For instance, *The Dictionary of Political Correctness* prohibits the eating of animals or anything that ever had a life, or wearing animal fur or skins. But it goes much further, even calling eggs, milk, wool, etc. "stolen products of voiceless victims." They recently deemed broccoli to be a living being with a nervous system.

What must be thoroughly frustrating is their strategy to rid the culture of anything Christian. They want to remove "In God We Trust" from our money, and government buildings to be stripped of any religious symbols. Recently, however, many so-called politically correct groups have welcomed the posting of Jewish and Muslim symbols while demanding the removal of nativity scenes.

In order to accomplish the removal of all Christian emblems from the public square, they must depend upon a Supreme Court whose halls are adorned with the Ten Commandments, and which opens each session with prayer. What a dichotomy! The court opens with a prayer for wisdom in determining whether that same God is allowed in the public discourse.

It is considered politically incorrect to cut down a tree, or to harm any species of animal that is "protected," and it is considered politically incorrect to execute the guilty and incorrigible in order to protect society. But it is considered politically correct to destroy an innocent child in the womb. And, this crowd tries to convince us that we have a "right" to abortion on demand. But, then, our rights, according to the Bill of Rights, are endowed by our Creator, who instructed us to subdue the earth and protect the little ones.

They can't seem to escape the God they strive to relegate to obscurity. If the Constitution were written today, it would be declared unconstitutional because of references to God, Creator, and the fact that it was signed "...in the year of our Lord." They have been largely successful in removing "Merry Christmas" as a greeting, substituting "Happy Holidays." They may as well find another greeting, because the word "holiday" comes from "Holy Day." A few years ago, many began substituting "Merry Xmas" for Christmas. The Greek symbol for Christ is the letter X. Back to the drawing board, PCs.

What about the states, counties, cities, streets, etc. with Christian-related names. It would bankrupt the country to try to change all of the road and street signs and remove all references to saints or Christian heritage. How does Corpse, Texas, sound, or simply Antonio, Texas, or Ignace, Michigan? You get my drift.

The Bible tells us in Proverbs, "There is a way which seems right to man, but in the end it leads to death." Many may argue that America was not founded as a Christian nation, but there is no doubt that Christ has had an insurmountable effect upon this culture and the world. People may try to remove Christ, but they are frustrated at every turn.

They even try to rewrite history to fit their agenda. "History," as in His Story? So many roadblocks, so little time...

SHAME MISSING IN
MEDIA APOLOGIES

During a Super Bowl half-time show, Janet Jackson experienced an "apparel malfunction" that launched a national conversation about censorship versus freedom of speech and expression. Fans of "shock jock" Howard Stern were incensed when he was fired by a group of radio stations because of vulgar and racial statements.

Many people believe that anything is acceptable over the public airways and that anyone who is offended by such transmissions or broadcasts can simply turn the station off. While it may be easy to make the decision to turn off a program such as Howard Stern once the listener is aware of the likely content, such action was not easy to make with the Janet Jackson debacle.

Like many other parents and grandparents, we watched the Super Bowl with our teenage grandson and a few of his friends. Past practice gave no indication that we needed to be poised to change the channel to avoid inappropriate viewing, although some of the costumes and movements of the background dancers made me consider doing so.

One should logically believe that a half-time show would be benign viewing for young and old. Such was not the case, but the ensuing weak apologies and excuses by the perpetrators were only exceeded by the gall of those who approved, even celebrated, the "performance." Weak remorse was expressed, and many people quickly came to the defense of all involved.

I often use controversial issues as learning tools for my children and grandchildren by encouraging them to view issues through God's morality. My grandson stated that if the incident was accidental, then why was there no evidence of shock, humiliation, or shame on the faces of any of those on the stage.

The lack of shame. In that observation, I think Christopher understood exactly what happened on television that Sunday evening. I'm afraid that the concept of shame is just another victim of the modern "new morality," a byproduct of political correctness. Tolerance of all that is immoral encourages us to look the other way when confronted with disturbing actions and words. It is now considered intolerant to expect people to live by any code that requires chastity or self-control.

Many of the God-given self-monitoring attributes like shame, modesty, self-restraint, etc., are today viewed as unnecessary infringements upon our media-driven quest for self-satisfaction at all costs. But, as we see quite often, those who live on the edge and ignore moral promptings usually end up in shame and disgrace as their excesses spill over into self-destructive, public humiliation.

It mostly boils down to a false self-image that insists that one is so good at what he does, or so physically beautiful, or so rich, that he is beyond the constraints of any moral code of conduct. Therefore, he believes he can violate moral standards and still be idolized by the masses.

When such activity becomes public and is abruptly placed before our eyes and ears without warning, we who believe in the traditional Judeo-Christian moral code must reject such concepts. They are the way of the world, and Christ would have us take a stand and refuse to be force-fed such indecency.

Christians know that we cannot change the world, but we do not have to join in worldly activities. We can bring God's word to all who we meet, and reflect Christ in our actions and words.

Instead of dwelling on self, we must think, as the book of Philippians says, on "whatsoever things are true, honorable, pure, lovely, praise worthy…" God honors such a demeanor.

WHO RAISED THESE KIDS?

A reporter traveling with the U.S. military in Iraq was moved nearly to tears by the unexpected selflessness of several soldiers. The reporter had received permission to allow three or four soldiers to use his international cellular phone to make short calls home. The first soldier he approached said he would rather allow his platoon leader, who has a pregnant wife at home, to have the talk time.

As the soldier trotted off to find his platoon leader, the reporter offered the phone to two other soldiers standing near by. Those soldiers declined the offer to call their own families, asking instead to use the talk time to call and comfort the parents of a fellow soldier who had recently been killed in battle. The reporter, caught off guard, exclaimed on the air, "Who raised such kids?" Who, indeed?

The same question could be asked about the young American men who were captured fighting with the Taliban in Afghanistan, or the young men who hijacked jets full of innocent civilians and slammed them into the World Trade Center towers and the Pentagon. Who reared those young (and perhaps a few not-so-young) men who thwarted the hijackers on Flight 93 by giving up their lives to keep the plane away from its intended destructive destination?

The answer, of course, is that decent, honorable, caring parents reared such young people. For every person who stands up and expresses his support for his child for protesting against America, or burning the flag, or fighting with the enemy, there are untold numbers of parents who, in the midst of their fear and apprehension, speak of their pride in their child who has taken up the challenge to serve.

Many parents fail to teach their children that there are some things worth fighting for. Many have allowed their children to grow up taking for granted all of the gifts and blessings that have been bestowed upon them undeservedly. Some parents take twisted pride in watching their children grow up as spoiled brats who believe they should always have their way, and that nothing is sacred or worthy unless it serves them. Those who fail to teach their young to honor God and to be thankful for their blessings often find that their children don't honor or respect them, either.

Another young man enlisted in the military for the sole reason of obtaining a free college education. It was peacetime, so he felt that this was the best way to get a free education then get out. When the Iraq war broke out, and his division was about to be activated, he filed for conscientious objector status, and requested a general discharge.

The military advised him that with a volunteer military the conscientious objector provision had no meaning, and he was obligated to complete his military pledge. He filed suit and was quickly supported by the ACLU and other organizations. Apparently, his parents never taught him to follow through on commitments.

Stories like the one about the soldiers' phone calls simply warm the heart and show that, in spite of the MTV, Jerry Springer, anti-American protestor culture, there are many parents who take seriously their responsibility to raise good citizens, and there are many young people who routinely make honorable, right life decisions, forgoing the dead-end cultural fads and choose to live their lives honorably.

Such honorable people aren't born that way. They are likely the product of parents who trust in God's promise, "Raise up a child in the way he should go, and when he is old he will not depart from it."

BLACK MEDIA STILL REFUSE TO PLACE BLAME WHERE IT BELONGS

A recent column by Cynthia Tucker, of *The Atlanta Constitution*, at first seemed to indicate that some blacks in leadership and the media have begun to see the light. Then, however, she went on to send mixed signals. For the sake of future generations, we hope change is coming.

Tucker wrote that the state of Georgia recently discovered young black men are in trouble: quitting school, fathering children out of wedlock, and dabbling in drugs and crime. She and others call for an intense outreach by parents, teachers, and churches to reverse stats that show that a third of young black men are or have been in jail, while only twenty-one percent of black males enter college.

But she assures us that she still defines success by increasing black college enrollment while disregarding dismal college grad levels and blames the "lingering effects of racism" for crime and failing grades. While few would disagree that racism does, and always will, exist in some measure, clearly, the major stumbling blocks facing today's black youth are placed there by bad life choices. She reports the symptoms clearly, but misses the point if she thinks placing unqualified Blacks in college programs simply to get the numbers up shows progress.

Still, we must take heart in any tiny steps the media elite take toward turning today's youth from their destructive path. So, Tucker's statement that as long as parents and others remain "…dismissive of serious academic (problems), black students will consign themselves to mediocrity, at best, or failure at worst. And no amount of affirmative action will change that," was both true and encouraging.

Many conservative columnists, myself included, have long warned about the self-destructive choices of young people, particularly young black men. But we have been castigated as being out of touch, deceived, or simply in denial of the rampant racism that blacks supposedly face today. Sadly, racism is used as a straw man to avoid blaming our own self-defeating actions and decisions for our problems.

Mainstream black leaders and their enablers in the dominant media have ignored the warnings and blasted those who entreat blacks to look within for answers. Journalists, such as Walter Williams and Thomas Sowell, have long warned that the destructive effect of rap music, dabbling in crime and drugs, and celebrating anti-social behavior were destroying the moral fiber of black society.

Anyone who speaks out against the practice of accusing Blacks who excel of "acting white," or who refuses to blame racism for the consequences of bad choices is considered a "sell-out" or simply "out of touch." Hopefully, Tucker's column reflects that black leaders and columnists are beginning to realize that most of today's black youth's problems stem from parents who refuse to properly discipline their children or insist on academic excellence. Those who set a positive example and insist that their children seek excellence usually see positive outcomes.

Effective results will be realized only after two major changes take place.

1. Black leaders must stop insisting upon quotas to fill academic slots based upon skin color, regardless of qualification. Instead, they should adhere to the original concept of Affirmative Action, i.e. applying the same standards to all candidates, affording all eligible candidates a fair exam and interview, and choosing the most qualified.

2. Black parents must stop blaming others for the consequences of bad choices, and resolve to give their youth a moral compass that leads them to, as the Bible says, "Avoid the passions of youth, and strive for righteousness, faith, love and peace, together with those who, with a pure heart, call out to the Lord for help."

LEARNING TO LIVE IN
AN "EMPTY NEST"

Family dynamics change dramatically after the kids leave home. The parent/grown child relationship differs greatly from the normal child/parent dynamics. Although it may be difficult for parents to believe, most young people do eventually leave home. Parents must then learn how to live all over again in what we call "The Empty Nest Syndrome," which my wife and I have experienced.

As each of our four daughters departed from our home, we faced certain adjustments, logistical (i.e. fights over the newly vacated bedroom), as well as emotional. After our youngest went away to college, we quickly entered The Syndrome.

Grocery shopping and food preparation were early manifestations of this syndrome. We continued to buy milk by the gallon, and subsequently threw most of it out. Even a half gallon proved to be too much, so we buy quarts. Invariably, one of our daughters will drop by and drink the available milk in one sitting.

We continued to cook enough food for four to six people. Old habits die hard. Another new experience: an abundance of leftovers. After about four nights of the same meatloaf on my plate, garnished in a vain attempt to disguise its familiarity, it was obvious that we needed to change our meal planning.

Actually, it was pretty neat. A smaller grocery list allowed us to buy the choice, individual potatoes and onions instead of buying by the sack. We could eat more steak and less pot roast, ground round rather than hamburger. We could also afford to eat out more often.

We quickly discovered the "Empty Nest Law": The smaller the meal, the more likely a grown progeny will show up at dinner time, looking gaunt and famished. This law taught us to keep "heat 'n' eat" food on hand, like hot dogs and burger patties, and to invite the "guest" to fix herself something else instead of coveting our plates.

Empty Nesters also find that, while pre-approved access to their kids' homes is not allowed, the kids insist on keeping keys to their parents' home. One daughter, frequently in need of cosmetics, clothing, and other necessities of life, would simply "shop" through her mother's closet, jewelry, and make-up when no one was home. After all, this will always be her "home," right? We took the key.

Parents are expected to leave the departed grown child's room the way it was left, perhaps as a safety net. One visiting daughter tearfully asked what we had done to "her room." I calmly responded, "Oh, you must mean my office. You didn't really expect us to leave that room like it was did you?" She did.

Not that we don't have enough reminders of our children. Our basement looks like a self-storage facility. I think we recently declared our fifth ultimatum, "If you don't

remove your stuff by (insert date), we will give it to charity."
I think they realize we're bluffing by now.

Nesters also are not to meddle in the business of their grown-up children, but the kids somehow retain the right to know your whereabouts. Returning from an impromptu weekend away, we found several terse phone messages, including, "Hey! It's after midnight. Where are you?" and "Didn't you guys come home at all last night? Why didn't you tell us you were going away? Call me as soon as you get home!" My how things change.

Many young adults' expectations of unbridled freedom from rules are quickly blindsided by brutal, blunt reality. Reality often breeds a longing for home sweet home. Grown children moving back in with their parents is a subject for another time.

When parents follow God's design for rearing children and teach their children that God commands them to, "Honor your father and mother…" parents and child enter into a new, exciting, and mutually fulfilling relationship with each other. Then, the nest is not so empty after all.

TODAY'S SCARY, INEFFECTIVE PARENTING CONCEPTS

A Nevada mom was arrested for leaving a baby in a car in summer heat to go gambling. A Midwest mother was arrested after a bystander saw her swat her kid on the bottom, and called the police. Both women were sentenced to attend "parenting classes."

While it certainly is appropriate to show a misguided parent the proper way to protect and discipline a child, a government-run "parenting class" sounds rather chilling. I contacted one program for more information. I was advised that parenting classes teach parents all areas of child rearing: changing diapers, potty training, discipline, decision-making, etc. I asked whether the instructors had successfully raised families of their own, and was told that most instructors are childless, single, and often recent college grads, but the entire staff, she assured me, were certified in the latest child-rearing methodology.

The program director said the most prevalent problem is improper parental discipline. "You wouldn't believe how many parents still don't realize that under no circumstances should spanking or hitting be used to discipline children," she said. "The second most frequent problem is not parents endangering children, but, rather parents who try to 'control' their children, which stifles self-expression." She dismissed my suggestion that there is a big difference between spanking in love to bring about correction, and beating, and that a parent who places gambling, drugs, or anything else ahead of a child's safety needs to first rid themselves of self-defeating personal behavior before they can benefit from parenting classes. She advised me that such an unenlightened approach to discipline is antiquated and not applicable in rearing children of the 90s.

The philosophy behind such programs promotes social engineering rather than effective parenting. Steeped in Secular Humanism, "corrective parenting" programs are the antithesis of traditional, proven child rearing steps. For instance, parenting experts believe spanking teaches a child to use violence to resolve conflict. Experts tell us to choose words that inspire the child to behave. When words don't work, the only acceptable recourse is to place the child in "time out" mode (during which the child typically either screams and trashes his room, or sulks defiantly). The Bible says, "He who spares the rod hates his son. But he who loves him disciplines him promptly." Today's social engineers have reversed this concept by teaching that love means never having to discipline a child. Discipline may, at once, be punitive (when required), corrective and instructive. It is terribly ineffective when any one of those approaches is used to the exclusion of the others.

Each new generation thinks it has created a "better way." Today's politically correct approach encourages moral degradation through music, print, and TV while frowning upon such concepts as personal integrity, accountability, and morality. Instead of parents guiding their children, many young simply drift through life with little or no direction, embracing any fad or counter-culture gimmick and making heroes of people who were once considered social outcasts. Dramatic increases in child crime, violence, irreverence, and immorality trumpet the failure of today's dominant philosophy that strives for "good feelings" rather than teaching children to be good.

In past generations, parents, teachers, and churches worked together to teach children to make proper life choices and to respect authority, which usually resulted in strong, honorable adults. Families sat around the dinner table (families rarely eat together today), where parents learned what was going on in their kids' lives. Is the child involved in inappropriate activity or violent/profane music? Who are his friends? Is he involved in illegal behavior or gangs? Children learned how to address life issues from their parents. Most parents knew their children so well that they could almost read their thoughts just by eye contact. Likewise, they could send a corrective message to a child across a crowded room. Today, the child appears to be in control more often than not.

Parenting is tough, but it's not the government's job. It's the parent's job to teach and discipline his children. Those who believe that discipline and moral absolutes should be avoided may have lots of book knowledge, but I'd rather depend upon the Book by the one who has infinite knowledge.

SOME PEOPLE NEED TO GET OUT MORE OFTEN

S ome of us need to get out and travel more often.

As a frequent traveler, I have found that one of the most pathetic sights to behold is an American in a foreign country demanding rights that he left at the U.S. border. American citizens who believe that living almost anywhere else in the world is preferable to living in the U.S. could not be further from the truth. America is truly the best place to live.

I wish American detractors could be offered free flights to the destination of their choice. U.S. rights such as freedom to speak our minds in public, or to redress our government when we disagree with its policies, are non-existent in much of the rest of the world.

If you are arrested or detained in America, you are allowed to have legal representation, which is provided free of charge if the you cannot afford it. In most other countries, you are fortunate to be allowed to have a lawyer present in court. Another precious right that is taken for granted is the presumption of innocence. In most countries, the accused is presumed to be guilty, and must prove his innocence. In America, the government must prove, beyond a shadow of doubt, that a defendant is guilty. Once found not guilty, a person cannot be charged again for the same crime. This is not the case in most of the world.

At U.S. Customs points of entry, signs explain that federal agents are required by law to check for illegal drugs, and that rude treatment by an agent should be reported to a supervisor. In the Republic of China, a bold sign simply states that possession of illegal drugs in China is punishable by death. In many countries, a person who is arrested may be held indefinitely. *Habeas corpus* laws, which require that the person be formally charged or released, do not exist outside in the U.S. Unless a defendant is a person of privilege, from a wealthy family, the chances of acquittal are slim in many nations.

Americans believe in "tolerance," and the freedom to believe and to act as one wishes. Many Americans are shocked to find that some other countries impose the death penalty for simply believing other than as prescribed by the government. In parts of India, people are paid to sit at the crossroads of villages to peer into passing vehicles to determine whether foreigners, specifically Christians, are entering the villages. Currently, Indian nationals are allowed to share their faith, but non-Indians are prohibited from visiting villages or homes.

One Indian-born college professor is listed as a "non-resident Indian" because he is a Christian who has lived outside India for several years. He is prohibited from visiting his mother's home or other relatives' homes, and is required to inform the police of his movements and lodging while in the country. Speaking out against the government is also punishable by death or imprisonment in much of the world outside the U.S.

Many American blacks have developed a romantic affinity for Africa, believing that their lot in life would be better in Africa than in the U.S. As one who spent many weeks in Africa, I know full well that I am blessed to have been born in America. Although I still correspond with many friends in Africa, there is no African country for which I would even consider giving up my American citizenship. To me, that would be tantamount to giving up my birthright, as Esau did in the book of Genesis.

My travels have made me even more thankful to be an American. Those who despise the fact that they were not born somewhere else really need to get out and travel more often.

WRITTEN IN THE STARS

One of today's state-of-the-art programs for honoring a loved one is to have a star named for him or her. The star, along with directions as to where to locate it in the heavens (with a telescope powerful enough to discern a specific star, no doubt), is then "registered" to the person, and shines for all time, in honor of the person for whom it was named.

As an old fashioned hopeless romantic, myself, far be it from me to disparage anyone's efforts to show love and affection for someone special to him. I get strange stares and comments because I often deliver roses to my wife for no special reason. It seems that many people believe that roses are only for special occasions or when one is "in the dog house."

I happen to believe flowers are more appropriate when one just wants to brighten the day of a loved one, or just to remind her that she is special and that you are thinking of her. I would suppose that naming a star for someone could serve the same purpose, although it would not be evident to others, and would require some effort to see it.

The main issue with such a gift, in my estimation, is

that one cannot give away that which doesn't belong to him. It may be a little more than irreverent to sell something that belongs to God Himself. The Bible proclaims that the heavens and earth belong to Almighty God. I don't believe God placed the stars in their places for advertisement or sales gimmickry, but rather, to spell out in the heavens the most important story in history.

According to Dr. D. James Kennedy, of Coral Ridge Ministries, in his book *The Real Meaning of the Zodiac*, the stars are not merely decorations for the night skies, but they tell the complete story of Creation, the fall of mankind, and salvation through the perfect life, sacrifice, death, and resurrection of Jesus Christ. Dr. Kennedy believes that mankind, in our sinful human nature, decided to use the symbols and star patterns in the heavens to tell stories about gods and mythical beings of our own creation. Dr. Kennedy goes through to illustrate, convincingly, that the stars in the heavens, "…declare the glory of God." He shows how each constellation, each grouping of stars and solar system, spell out the incredible love of mankind by an all-knowing, all seeing and gracious God, through His Holy Spirit, and to the glory of His only Son, Jesus Christ.

While naming a star for another person may be a cute gesture, it is more honorable to show love and respect to all of our neighbors on a daily basis. The Lord would rather we spend our time making sure that our loved ones know Him and have a personal relationship with Christ. God wants us to focus on living a godly, chaste life that is under control and listening to His Holy Spirit for daily guidance.

Rather than having a star with my name on it, God wants me to be one of His shining stars, bringing His light to the world. Philippians 2:14 says, "Do everything without grumbling and arguing, *so* that you may be blameless and pure, children of God who are faultless in a crooked and perverted generation, among whom you shine like stars in the world." It is more comforting to me to know that my name is written in the Book of Life because of Christ's free gift of eternal life, than to have a star that I will never see and that cannot save me, named for me.

THE BLESSINGS OF
PERSECUTION

When did Christmas become a bad word? And when did Christianity become something to be loathed and feared? No one knows for sure, some point to a 1989 lawsuit by the ACLU against a county for violating the separation clause of the Constitution by lighting a Christmas tree on government property, so they now raise a "Holiday tree," with no problem.

All over the country, we now have holiday celebrations with parades and all manner of fictitious characters, except the One for whom the holiday came into existence. During my many years as an administrator, I never had a non-Christian employee ask to work on Christmas Day. Sadly, those who would like to remove any vestige of Christianity from our culture seem to be having some success. We are told that the founders of this nation intended to avoid any mention of religion, yet, when one reads the very words of the founders, it is clear that most were active Christians. The Declaration of Independence and the Preamble to the Constitution both allude to a Creator.

Daily, we hear stories of attempts to shut Christ out of every area of public and private life. Some have sued to remove "In God We Trust" from our coins and currency (one of the groups seems to be having trouble raising money for its cause). There is also a lawsuit to prohibit the recitation of the Pledge of Allegiance in schools, because it includes "...under God..."

These days, many feel it is okay to castigate anyone who is "openly" Christian. We who "let our lights shine" are labeled Holy Rollers, fanatics and religious zealots. Some Christians have been threatened with imprisonment for espousing their beliefs. Coaches and school officials have found themselves in jeopardy of losing their jobs, and possibly going to jail for allowing students or athletes to participate in prayer.

Christians should not take such persecutions personally. The venom is not intended for us, but is aimed at the Lord. Christians, when confronted by a challenge to their Christian beliefs, should simply respond by praying for the unbeliever. They cannot change the person, but the Holy Spirit can. The Lord does not need us to fight His battles or to confront people. We are to show them Christ's love by all that we say or do. That is when God's power works best in the life of an unbeliever.

Many years ago, churches started small group or "cell group" ministries, whereby several members would meet regularly in homes to sing and praise the Lord and spend time in His word. This type of small group ministry was intended to show Christians ways to get together and worship in case the day came when church gatherings were prohibited. At the time, such a prohibition seemed impossible, but, today, sadly, it doesn't seem so far fetched.

We can, however, take heart because Jesus Himself told

us to be happy when these things happen. In the fifth chapter of Matthew He tells us, "Blessed are you when people insult you, persecute you and falsely say all kinds of evil against you for my sake. Rejoice and be exceedingly glad, because great is your reward in Heaven, for in the same way they persecuted the prophets who were before you." Take heart, Christians. Christ has it under control.

SEEKING SHARING OPPORTUNITIES AROUND THE WORLD

I have had the opportunity to travel much of the world during the past twenty-five years, beginning with a month-long trip to Africa in the early eighties to my most recent trip in October 2005 to Sri Lanka and India. It is amazing how often I have found myself sharing my faith with others as I travel.

I traveled to Sri Lanka during October and early November, 2005, with a team tasked with rebuilding an orphanage destroyed by the tsunami on December 26, 2004, and to issue eyeglasses. Many of the people had either lost theirs in the giant wave, or never had the means to obtain them. The second phase of the trip was to Trivandrum, in southern India, to conduct planning for a group called Passiton, India.

Local politics prohibited the rebuilding segment, but we examined more than 2,000 people and issued more than 1,600 pairs of glasses. The recipients were overwhelmed with gratitude. But some of the people wondered out loud why their God would bring such grief upon them, in spite of their faithful worship life and hard work.

Such conversations opened opportunities to talk to them about a loving Lord who died to pay for our sins, for which we cannot pay, and offers us eternal life. We take care not to denigrate their beliefs, but we take the opening to talk about ours, and to explain how sin came into the world, and brought with it disasters and pain.

People in other countries are extremely interested in the American culture, and often ask questions ranging from family structure, to our eating habits, to our religious beliefs. In Taiwan, a young woman who worked in a Buddhist temple asked me about being a Christian in America. She inquired as to how the Buddhists and Christians got along here. She seemed shocked when I told her that there are very few Buddhist temples in America.

She wanted to know more about what we believed, and actually invited us to have tea right in the office area of the temple, where we shared the love of Christ and His offer of eternal life. She asked us to pray with her that she could obtain this precious gift. We did as she asked, and when I left Taiwan, she was regularly attending Bible studies and worship with a local Christian group.

During a trip to India, a man at a Hindu temple showed us the "Dead god tree" outside the temple. He explained that an item that is no longer useful as a god is brought to the temple and placed on the ground around this tree. He asked if Christians have such a tree. I explained that we have no need for such a tree, because our God doesn't die, but is eternal. As one friend of mine said, "Jesus would say, 'Been there, done that.'"

I presented the Gospel message, which he found interesting, but he was afraid to pray to receive Christ's free gift, for fear of losing his family and friends. One who converts to Christianity is shunned and considered dead. But a seed was planted. Many Hindus have received the saving grace of the Gospel message, and have found that God provides them with a new family of friends and associates.

I believe that wherever I am, whether traveling abroad or running an errand to the store, it is most important to be ready and willing to share my faith. Romans, 1:16 says, "For I am not ashamed of the Gospel, because it is God's power for salvation to everyone who believes…"

The Lord commands that every Christian share His message of salvation. If we are unafraid, the Holy Spirit will give us the words to say.

IT'S WHAT'S INSIDE
THAT COUNTS

C lothes make the man," was a prominent advertising slogan many years
ago. But do clothes really make a person better or more valuable?

It seems that today, there is a heightened fashion sense
among Americans. Men, who traditionally viewed a complete wardrobe as lots of "knock around" casual clothes, a
Sunday-go-to-meeting suit and clean underwear, some tennis shoes and a pair of dress shoes, seem to be as concerned
about being current on the latest fashion trends as women.

Businesses, and even churches, often relax dress policies to fit the more casual lifestyles of people today. Casual
Fridays are the norm, and many churches advertise a "come
as you are" atmosphere, at which jeans, shorts and other
casual attire is welcomed. It seems to fit well with the trend
toward less rigid rules and more permissiveness in many
areas of life.

I personally prefer to wear a suit and tie whenever I
attend church. It seems to put me in the mindset for worship. I would feel as uncomfortable wearing a suit and tie

on a fishing trip as I would wearing jeans and sneakers to church. It's not as much a spiritual issue with me, but comes from my upbringing. We had church clothes, school clothes, and play clothes, and rarely intermingled them with different activities.

Dress-up clothing traditionally cost more than casual clothing, but today, a pair of what used to be called "gym shoes" can easily cost more than a Sunday suit. In addition, one pair of sports shoes will no longer work for all sports. A visit to a shoe store will reflect that there are special shoes for basketball (often endorsed by a player, which multiplies the cost), for running, walking, tennis, etc.

It seems that people, young and old, spend an inordinate amount of time stressing over having the latest and most expensive wardrobe available, from head to toe. The fashion industry dutifully changes styles to keep up with the ever-changing latest, hottest (now called "phatest") fashions. Try to find men's jeans that are not four sizes larger than the tag shows, and that have belt loops included, and you will understand what I mean.

Even small children seem to want to be seen with the latest and most expensive styles available. Modern media, especially TV, can instantly conjure up intense covetousness in an entire generation in one fell swoop by expounding on the latest fashion "must have" item. TV commercials and sitcoms preach a never-ending mantra to young minds that to be the best you must wear the latest fashions. The sale of acne medications is through the roof, because young people believe that any spot or blemish renders one less than acceptable.

If only such emphasis were placed upon developing good moral character. If only people looked for godly, honest people to admire, rather than the people who demonstrate the greatest lack of responsibility in their lives.

The Lord could care less how we look on the outside, or how many imperfections we can cover up, or how many of today's fashions we can adorn ourselves with. He entreats us to ask Him through His Holy Spirit, to create in us clean hearts and right spirits.

The Bible tells us, "... for the LORD seeth not as man seeth; for man looketh on the outward appearance, but the LORD looketh on the heart." It is more important that He sees a clean heart in me, rather than stylish, meaningless clothing on the outside.

REFUSAL TO FORGIVE HAS
BOOMERANG EFFECT

I recently heard a person say, "I will never forgive him for what he did!" All too often, people feel so hurt or offended that they do not believe the offending person deserves forgiveness. Many people believe such a declaration to be profound, valiant, or courageous. Refusing to forgive another is often used to underscore the disdain the speaker holds for someone who may have done something despicable and cruel against him or a loved one.

Perhaps the declarer believes that refusing to forgive an offense locks the offender into a state whereby he or she is condemned to suffer forever. Or perhaps it sends the offender into some type of inescapable purgatory as penance for his actions. Or maybe the thought of someone holding a grudge against him haunts him daily. Probably not.

Does your unforgiving demeanor place a psychological chain around the wrongdoer's neck as a constant reminder that you will never forget the offense? Not likely. Some people believe that, in order to forgive a person who has hurt you, that person must ask for forgiveness and/or make restitution.

Surprisingly, refusal to forgive another person actually has the opposite effect. Living in a state of un-forgiveness may well trap the non-forgiving person in a place of bondage, while having little or no effect upon the offender. Refusal to forgive someone else requires one to own the hateful, spiteful feelings that accompany the state of un-forgiveness. The offence must be recalled and renewed and dwelled upon each time that person comes to mind. The emotional chains intended for the offender become a prison for the unforgiving person.

Psychologists and counselors often find it impossible to make much progress with a patient unless and until the person deals with past hurts and offenses perpetrated by others. Often, emotional roadblocks to healing are a by-product of the patient's refusal to forgive and let go of the anguish that automatically arises when he tries to hold on to a hurt or transgression he has suffered. One physician stated that the problem is exacerbated if the wrongdoer is deceased. The patient is often left with the despair of having no object of his hatred, which seems to cause that hatred to turn inwardly.

The Bible includes numerous passages dealing with forgiveness, so the concept must be very important for our spiritual well being. In Jeremiah, God told us that, if we repent of our sins, He would forgive our wrongdoing and never again remember our sin. A scientific study revealed that a person remembers only a fraction of his words and deeds; therefore, it is impossible to repent for everything.

Christ resolved the problem of having to remember and specifically repent for each individual bad thought, word or deed. He came to our rescue; living a perfect life, and offering himself as the perfect sacrifice for all of our sins, and offering Heaven as a free gift to those who receive it.

He included this important concept in the Lord's Prayer ("Forgive us our trespasses, as we forgive those who trespass against us ..."). However, He warns us in Matthew 6, "For if you forgive people their wrongdoings, your heavenly Father will forgive you as well. But, if you don't forgive people, your Father will not forgive your wrongdoing."

Take a moment and say a prayer of forgiveness for each and every offense committed against you. Where possible, follow up by personally asking offenders for forgiveness. Whether it is accepted or not is immaterial. If they're no longer alive, forgive them anyway. You will release yourself from the bondage of un-forgiveness and open the door to your Father's blessed forgiveness.

WHO WILL REHABILITATE NATE?

Nathaniel Abraham, at eleven years old, shot and killed Ronnie Green, Jr. At thirteen, he was sentenced to juvenile detention. The judge ruled that rehabilitation, not punishment, was more appropriate for a young kid. The problem is that at age twenty-one, Nate will be released regardless of whether rehabilitation has taken place.

Nate (with a crime history dating to age eight) is in dire need of rehabilitation. His mind and heart need renewal, and his focus changed. But more likely, Nate will just be ware-housed, without any semblance of "rehabilitation," returning to society tougher and more out of control than when he went in.

So who will rehabilitate Nate? The hand-wringers who weep for this child they label a victim? Will they go to the jail to mentor and guide this child toward making better life decisions and choices? No, they won't. They'd rather "curse the darkness than light a candle of hope."

What about his mother, who says she begged in vain for help as Nate accumulated more than twenty encounters with the police. Had she told the authorities that she intended to spank the boy, swift and sure action would have taken place! Psychological tests show that Nate is not mentally ill, but suffers arrested development from lack of structure and direction in his young life. And his mom doesn't feel responsible.

How about the psychologists? Will they rehabilitate Nate? No. The current approach to anti-social behavior is to blame society, the police, poor potty training, racism, or anything except the guilty party. Maybe the black leaders stepped in and demonstrated for Nate's release with no punishment. Not likely. These leaders apply a litmus test to every moral decision to assure that it serves their agenda before they take any action. For instance, both Nate and his victim were black. Had Nate been white, Green would have been given martyr status. But instead he has been largely ignored; sacrificed in favor of Nate, who is a more valuable tool by which to heap guilt upon society and give relevance to these self-serving leaders.

Will society insist that Nate receive the treatment, training, supervision, and guidance needed to change his world view and turn him around? No. Sadly, we simply will all go on with our lives, smugly believing we have done the right thing by not sentencing this "victim" as an adult. And since Nate is now a ward of the state, ministerial guidance would probably violate the so-called separation of church and state.

All of these approaches to rehabilitation fall woefully short, largely because they leave out a very important element—personal accountability. The judge chose a "blended sentence" rather than send a young kid to an adult prison to be victimized. But by failing to "blend" some personal accountability into the sentence, he probably did Nate a very serious disservice. Since the sentence placed no mandate on Nate other than incarceration, he may refuse schooling, counseling, therapy, or any other rehabilitation attempts. The sentence is devoid of accountability, thereby precluding anyone from forcing Nate to do anything. If Nate commits no serious felony in jail, he will simply walk out at age twenty-one. The only certainty will be his return to a life of crime.

What the Nates of today need most is what they are so staunchly "protected" from—their Savior. The Bible says, in Mark 10, children were brought to Christ for Him to touch them, and He said, "Let the little children come to me, and do not forbid them, for of such is the kingdom of Heaven."

Christ has the healing touch, and had Nate been brought to Him, it is unlikely that he would be where he is today. Nothing else can rehabilitate like His love. Pray that Nathaniel will receive Christ, who truly rehabilitates, in his life.

THE JONAH SYNDROME

Many of us have been afflicted with, "The Jonah Syndrome." Jonah was a prophet who refused God's command to go and prophesy to the people of Nineveh. Instead, Jonah ran away and boarded a ship. God fed him to a great fish. After being spat out onto the land, Jonah delivered the message to Nineveh. We often experience this syndrome. While God doesn't use such dire circumstances as a hungry fish to get our attention, He does use His own miraculous means to get us to pay attention and follow His course for our lives.

One example of this is Pastor Dean. He never consciously refused God's call, nor did he literally hear God speak. But he often felt a small voice, leading him and encouraging him at each juncture of his life, but giving no discernable, specific direction. Dean grew up in a loving, Christian family in the farming community of Frankentrost, Michigan. After college, he joined the U.S. Navy, spending significant time on a submarine. Dean talks about the unending boredom and quiet time on board. All the time for introspection did not reveal his life's direction, but the small voice was often there.

After the Navy, Dean became an electrical contractor. In both the Navy and his business, he learned how to deal with difficult people, and learned to seek God's perspective in all circumstances through Bible study and prayer. That small voice whispered. It was easy to ignore at first, but, eventually he had little doubt the Lord was trying to tell him something. Dean grew tired of struggling with his inability to discern God's will, so he made the decision to enroll in seminary out of weariness. It was after he made the decision that he finally had peace and understood that he was being led to a life of service to Christ.

Dean graduated from seminary and became a Lutheran minister. He finally felt the peace of knowing that he was where he was supposed to be. He now uses the wealth of life experiences to encourage, admonish, and lead the flock that God has entrusted in him. One parallel to Jonah could be that God placed Dean inside a man-made "fish," where he had plenty of time to "be still" and hear God's voice, as the Lord carefully knit in Dean's heart the fabric of his desire for Dean to have a life of service to Him.

Another example is "Terry," who grew up in the rebellious 1960s, and lived a life that was typically loose and unstructured. Prayer life was not a priority. Terry also heard God's small voice many times in his life, but was largely disinterested in "churchy" things. One day, Terry was badly burned in a flash fire. God had placed him in a situation where he had to "Flee to God's boundless mercy" for peace and healing. Terry eventually heard God's voice loud and clear. He prayed to receive Christ as his Lord and Savior. He was blessed with a very successful contracting business, and he dedicated both his business and personal life to Christ. God blessed him with a wonderful wife and family. Life was *good*. Terry, however, still could hear that small voice, even though he lived a life of worship, regularly participating in and leading prayers both in church and in his business associations. God showed Terry a great void that existed in the community of builders, contractors, and other business people. Eventually, Terry was led to go into the ministry, and today leads Commerce church, which ministers to business people and others. Terry's "fish" may have been the fire that engulfed and nearly killed him.

We all experience our "Jonah" moments, when we simply tune God out and ignore His direction for our lives. Sometimes He uses extreme circumstances to get our attention. Sometimes, He closes each door as we approach it, until the only direction left is His direction. Sometimes, the "fish" appears as a state of despair and loneliness. He only wants us to be in tune to His will through his Word, and to listen and "Be still, and know that I am God," and to declare His wonderful gift of eternal life to others.

SHOULD CHRISTIANS
FOLLOW CURRENT EVENTS?

There are many people today who rarely, if ever, read the newspaper or watch TV news because it contains nothing but trash, or because it glamorizes crime and degradation, or because it offers little of redeeming social value. While I agree that we often need some kind of antiseptic to cleanse our ears and minds after viewing, reading, or listening to most news programs, I also believe that responsible people should know what is happening in our world.

People shun news reports for various reasons; they don't like the "spin" that is put on it, or they don't believe that moral people should fill their minds with the filth, corruption, and secular views and trends of the world. Many Christians believe that God would prefer they not expose themselves to much of what is reported as news. That may not be completely true.

Quite often, people cite biblical and moral bases for not exposing themselves to the news, but they often find themselves shocked and embarrassed when dangerous concepts, trends, or legislation gain a foothold in their community right under their noses. They also find themselves victimized by gossip or a deliberately erroneous slant on major subject matter. Where moral issues are concerned, to be forewarned is to be forearmed. Psalms 112, states, "The righteous have no fear of bad news. His heart is steadfast in the Lord." We should want to be aware of the plans and actions of those immoral and unethical elements which have gained so much power and influence in today's society. Sometimes a little "righteous indignation" is the only thing that motivates good people to take a stand before evil manifests itself. Righteous indignation after the fact is not nearly as effective.

Christians must watch for ungodly or socially dangerous concepts so as to take steps to keep the enemy of all that is good from gaining momentum and support. God tells us that we should be cognizant of what goes on around us. Proverbs 27 says, "The prudent see danger and take refuge, but the simple keep going and suffer for it." Taking refuge may be as simple as educating ourselves as to potential problems in order to know what to pray about, or knowing when we should be gathering together with others who have the same values to resist some wrong law that is about to be foisted upon the public.

God also tells us that evil flourishes when good people do nothing. I'm not suggesting that you punish yourself by reading every daily newspapers or watching news channels all day. Nor am I suggesting that you allow the mainstream media to dictate your position on issues. I do believe, however, that we should all pay more attention to what's going on by watching and listening to the news and researching pertinent issues for ourselves. Then, we must be willing to delineate right from wrong, from God's perspective, and stand up and be counted when our basic beliefs and values are challenged. Think about it.

JUST WHO'S FLYING THIS THING, ANYWAY?

We've all seen those bumper stickers which proudly proclaim, "God Is My Co-Pilot!" Actually, flying is an excellent metaphor for our "flight" through life. It's relatively easy to picture life's journey as a flight from point A (birth), to point B (death). What happens between these two events can make for a good flight or a disastrous trip.

Sometimes we fly alone, making our own decisions, doing things that are clearly wrong and simply calling our own shots. The problem with flying alone is that we are imperfect creatures, and we neglect to accept the helping hand when it is offered, and we suffer the consequences of our bad decisions. Our lack of ability to solve our problems or avoid consequences causes us despair. Despair leads to depression, which often leads to spiritual (or literal) death.

Sometimes, we fly on "automatic pilot," meandering aimlessly through life with no clear direction, no moral anchor to keep us on an even keel, and no one in whom we are willing to place our trust. Whatever comes our way, we try to ignore, excuse, or compromise our way around it. We don't take responsibility for our actions, because everything is the automatic pilot's fault. We are victims of fate, or bad potty-training, racism, an evil plot, etc.

But most of the time, each of us operates as the "pilot" of our life. The pilot is the one who takes and maintains control of the vessel, except on the occasion that he decides to relinquish control due to fatigue, or when he believes everything is under control. Actually, the same criteria often determines whether the pilot turns over control of the plane to the automatic pilot or to the co-pilot. The only difference is that the automatic pilot cannot make determinations or decisions, or respond to orders from air traffic controllers as the co-pilot can. Even so, the co-pilot must ask permission of the pilot (except under emergency circumstances) to alter any of the elements of the established flight plan.

When one considers the full implication of God as life's co-pilot, it is clear that, while the bumper stickers are intended to give God a place of honor, it actually relegates Him to barely above passenger status. In many cases, He is even limited to that status in our lives. A passenger, of course, is not allowed or invited to participate in any of the decisions involving the operation of the aircraft. He simply goes where the plane goes.

As our co-pilot, we often expect God to sit silently along side of us, waiting for the chance to participate in life's choices and decisions. God wants to be more than a co-pilot, who cleans up our mistakes, or takes over after we have tired of running things, or have made such a mess that we have no other place to look for help. When we allow the Lord to sit on the throne of our life, we can feel safe and know that many obstacles, tears, and fears will be avoided. God ordains our paths and knows the end of our life journey before it even begins.

The Bible, in Isaiah 58, says, "The Lord will guide you always." God knows us better than we know ourselves. He created us, and redeems us, and He wants to give us an abundant life here on earth in addition to eternal life through His son Jesus Christ. When I sit at the controls of my life, with God in a backup role, I am honoring myself and dishonoring Him. When I make decisions from my own sinful human perspective, my plans will always fail. But when I get out of the way, and allow God's Holy Spirit to guide each step of the way, I can rest assured that my life here on earth will be filled with joy and peace, and the Triune God gets the glory He so richly deserves. It all comes down to whom you are trusting with your life here on earth and on the other side of the grave. God is my pilot, and I trust Him with my life!

THE NEXT TIME
YOU SEE JESUS

A recent caller to a radio program reported seeing Jesus Christ walking down the street, barefoot and wearing a long white robe and carrying a cross. This sparked a plethora of callers from all over the Midwest claiming to have seen Jesus walking around. One person said he saw Jesus being arrested. One claimed to have seen him in Kalamazoo, Michigan, having lunch with Elvis.

Throughout history, people have reported sightings of Jesus. Some even relay messages to mankind, supposedly from Jesus. Even evangelist Oral Roberts once insisted that a nine hundred foot tall Jesus had appeared to him.

One caller who had not seen Jesus herself, had a message for anyone who might, "The next time you see Jesus," she began. "Tell him that I have some questions for him, like why he allows wars and murders, disasters and mistreatment of children. Why does he allow people to be poor and to experience serious illness and disease?"

Obviously, people who really believe that the next time they see Jesus, he will be walking among us, oblivious to all of the sin and chaos in the world, along with those who believe they will have their chance to confront the Redeemer of the world about the sins of mankind, have lot to learn from the Word of God.

First, the Bible tells us that evil resides in the hearts of humankind, and our hearts spout all manner of wickedness, including murder, theft, and hatred. Illness and disease exist in the world because sin exists in the world. Poverty is a relative term. In the U.S., there are people who are poor in spite of trying as hard as they can to eke out an existence. But, there are many "voluntarily poor," whose poverty stems from the consequences of their life choices and decision.

In many poor countries, powerful leaders prohibit the production of food, and withhold foreign aid and relief food in order to keep the masses under control. The late Jim Russell and Jim Dyet, authors of the book *Overcoming Subtle Sins,* opine that the subtle sin of greed feeds on materialism. If everyone obeyed God's commandment to love one another as we love ourselves, greed would not exist.

In Matthew chapter 24, Jesus goes into great detail to lay out what the world will be like when He returns. He gives signs to watch for, many of which clearly exist today. He tells us that, just as in Noah's day, people will go on with life; partying, marrying, and seeking as much gusto out of life as possible. He warns us that many false prophets and others will falsely come in His name. He tells us that families will battle against each other.

He even tells us exactly what we will witness when we see Him again. Matthew 24:30 says, "Then the sign of the Son of Man will appear in the sky, and then (all the earth) will mourn; and see the Son of Man coming on the clouds of Heaven with power and glory."

The Bible says that when Christ comes again to gather up those who trust in Him, He will not come humbly, or quietly walk around our cities and towns. Those who think they will confront Him and place the blame for our sins upon Him will be greatly surprised. Christ has already "been there, done that." He took the punishment for every one of man's wrongs, paid the price, and offers eternal life to anyone who will simply accept the free gift.

No. There will be no humility in Him when He returns. Every knee shall bow and every tongue will confess that Jesus Christ is Lord the next time we see Jesus!

WORTH THE PAPER
IT'S WRITTEN ON?

We've all received mail telling us that we have already won some fabulous prize—vacation, money, a new car. I recently received such a notice. I have learned from experience that such announcements rarely are authentic, and the truth usually resides in the small print.

The announcement began with tiny letters that stated, "If you return the winning entry, and meet other contest criteria, we will announce…" followed by the bold declaration that I had already won. It seems that many guarantees and warrantees today fall short of their promises.

Small print and deceptive wording is often used to convince us that we should sign up for a contest in which the main purpose is to force us to purchase unending books or magazines, or to sign a contract that is nearly impossible to rescind. Creative word usage often masks the unreliability of the "guaranteed" product, service, or contest. I once heard a story about a man who bought clothing "guaranteed to be shrink resistant." When he returned the garment—in miniature form—the clerk pointed out that "shrink resistant" means the garment will shrink, "but it doesn't like to."

In many cases, a guarantee is voided even through normal use of the product. I once bought a car tire with a 60,000 mile warrantee against factory defects. When a manufacturing defect developed at 30,000, the warrantee is prorated, accordingly, and I was required to pay fifty percent of the price of a replacement. One woman's new car warranty was voided after her vehicle blew a head gasket at 5,000 miles. The dealer determined that the radiator cap was faulty, which caused the thermostat to malfunction, and the resulting internal pressure in the engine caused the head gasket to blow. The warranty didn't cover thermostats or pressure caps. $1,500, please.

Once, out of curiosity, I responded to a letter that told me to pack my bags because I was the guaranteed winner of a totally free, all expense paid Caribbean vacation. When I called the number listed, the first thing I was asked for was my credit card number. They explained that the trip was totally free, but that either a credit card number or a $500 non-refundable deposit was required up front.

The increasing lack of integrity seems to flourish in many areas of today's society, and warranties and guarantees are some of the most prevalent offenders. Conditions, legalese, small print, and outright deceptive and misleading information abounds. One wonders whether there is any warranty or guarantee that is worth the paper it is printed on. The good news is that there certainly is!

There is one guarantee that is good for life—eternal life. Most people are familiar with John 3:16, "For God so loved the world that He gave His only begotten Son, that whoever believes in Him should not perish but have everlasting life," but the Holy Scripture also says in 1 John 5:13, "These things I have written to you who believe in the name of the Son of God, that you may know that you have eternal life." It doesn't leave us guessing whether we have eternal life. It doesn't include small print nor conditions. The guarantee doesn't expire, and you can't do anything to earn it. It is a free gift. The criminal who was being crucified with Christ simply showed repentance for his sins and asked Jesus for mercy. There was no time to go back and do a mountain of good, or to perform any rituals or service, yet, Christ told the man that he would, that day, be with him in paradise.

The guarantee offered by our Savior has no strings attached, is truly unconditional, and is available to all who will receive it.

CHRISTIAN MARTYRDOM

In January 2004, Pastor Mukhtar, a Christian minister in Pakistan, was gunned down on his way to visit his daughter. In southern India in 2005, a priest was shot and his church building was burned to the ground, reportedly by local Hindus who had warned him against leading Christian worship. The monthly magazine, *Voice of the Martyrs,* tells of numerous incidences of abuse, destruction, and even death among Christian ministers and evangelists spreading the Gospel message in countries around the world. Many countries prohibit the practice of Christianity, and often, preaching the Gospel is punishable by death. Still, God inspires and sends His messengers forth.

As a missionary, I have often been asked why I would risk harm to travel to sometimes hostile areas of the world to share my faith. I take no credit for being courageous or brave; in fact, I have often been frightened at first. But the simple answer is that Christ commanded me to do so. Also, I believe others have a need and a right to know about a Savior who can give them eternal life.

Prior to a recent missionary venture, I was asked whether I was worried about dying "over there." First, I told the person that if God wants to take me to Heaven, He can do it from inside my house, in my car, or overseas, and that I just trust that He will protect me, and bring me safely home. (Home could be back in the U.S. or in Heaven.)

More importantly, we don't go into the mission field alone. We have the assuring presence of the Holy Spirit. Also, Christ Himself has already warned us of what we may face. In The Great Commission, He told us to go out into the world and teach others to obey all that He has taught us. But, in Matthew 10:16, He warns us, "I am sending you out like sheep among wolves…" He further warns us that we may be harmed, and face arrest, torture, and even death.

He also puts death by martyrdom into perspective, when He told us, "Do not be afraid of those who kill the body but cannot kill the soul. Rather, be afraid of the One who can destroy both soul and body in hell." In the Beatitudes, He promises us that, when we are persecuted for His sake, He will greatly reward our efforts.

Many people opine that there are so many people right here in America who need to know about God's love. But the Lord doesn't see man's borders or national differences. He only sees sinners headed for eternal destruction, for whom He died to pay the perfect price for those sins, and offers eternal paradise to those who simply trust in Him. He wants to use us to go where He sends us, and simply tell others. His Holy Spirit travels with us and actually does all of the real work. The Holy Spirit enters into the person, creating faith, without which they cannot believe or understand the Gospel message.

Many times, I have witnessed the work of the Spirit as people seem to be transformed before our eyes, and who seemed to hunger for the message we brought to them.

Sometimes, a missionary does not have the opportunity to share the Gospel message, but simply shares God's love with others. Sometimes, a seed is planted, which, in God's time, will come to fruition. The Lord doesn't always answer our questions. He only asks us to be available wherever He sends us, and He does the rest.

HARRIET TUBMAN WOULD
FEAR JESSE JACKSON

The Underground Railroad helped countless slaves escape to the northern United
States and Canada. It was a treacherous
journey staying one step ahead of the slave hunters who
were paid by the Masters to bring back the escapees. These
slaves had never ventured beyond the boundaries of the
plantation on their own. Harriet Tubman, the leader of the
Underground Railroad, taught them to travel at night, and
how to discern which people were willing to help from those
who would turn them in for the bounty.

The people who instilled the most dread in escaped
slaves were the "overseers." Every plantation had overseers,
whose job was to keep the slaves in line, mete out beatings
and whippings at the master's whim, and to help capture,
return, and punish those who dared escape. Once recaptured,
the offending slave would be beaten, horse whipped, and tortured, sometimes to the point of death before the assembled
slaves. If the death of a captured slave served as a warning to
the others, then it was a good investment for the master.

The overseer was treated very well for his allegiance.

He was given better housing, food and clothing. He wasn't required to work the fields, but guarded those who did. But he was harshly treated when a slave failed to toe the line, and was often held personally liable if one escaped. He was to make sure that the slaves didn't learn to read, write, or entertain an original thought. The masters knew full well that education would provoke thoughts of freedom.

Fast forward to today. So-called leaders like Jesse Jackson and Al Sharpton are like overseers. They do everything they can to keep blacks from excelling. They convince blacks that they cannot make it on their own, but must depend upon these leaders to get money and programs from the government for them. Then, these leaders present these dumbed-down, initiative-starved people to corporations and foundations as "victims." The corporations and foundations then give millions to these overseers, which they keep for themselves. In return, they "deliver" the votes and allegiance of ninety percent of blacks. Any entity that refuses to be shaken down in this manner is labeled racist.

Any black person who refuses to wear the victim label, but who succeeds by playing by the rules and working hard, is labeled a "sell-out." Condoleeza Rice has achieved one of the highest levels of government through her own initiative, even though she came from meager beginnings. She was related to one of the little girls who died in the 60s arson fire in a Baptist church in Birmingham, so she knew racism, but she refused to let it stop her, and worked hard to excel. This put her at odds with the overseers, because she wouldn't wear the victim label, and was the antithesis of the belief that bigotry and racism prohibits blacks from excelling.

Colin Powell, Walter Williams, Thomas Sowell, and countless other blacks have likewise excelled without the help of the overseers, and they are scorned for having done so. They are called "Uncle Tom," when those who serve as overseers better fit that description. These people who have taken advantage of the blessings available in America cannot be driven back to the plantation, so they are written off by the overseers and their masters.

The true leaders lead by example. They do more to make a difference in the lives of this generation and the next by showing them that they don't have to be victims, that they don't have to give in to bad behavior, and that no one can hold them back but themselves. They show young people that they can do more than wring their hands, look backward at past injuries, and expect a bigot behind every tree.

They show blacks that what keeps many of them in bondage are bad decisions and choices, and following the overseers, rather than choosing rugged individualism. Each person holds the key to his success.

THE FINE ART OF SURRENDER

We, as a nation, seem to be in a dangerous "surrender" mode. We don't require excellence in academics, work, or even in sports. Children's sports are often made competition-free, with no winners or losers. Sometimes, the losing team is given an equal number of points to protect their self-esteem.

The result is kids who won't strive for excellence because someone will make up the shortfall. Those who do strive to excel are shown that, no matter how hard one tries, someone else can be as successful with little or no effort at all. So why try? We have ignored or castigated those who have decried the "dumbing down" of society. When academic excellence was replaced by "social promotion," whereby a student who fails in required subjects is elevated to the next grade, we sat quietly by. So many bizarre problems resulted, that social promotion is being quietly dismantled. Its proponents are not held accountable for the damage. They are still sought after for answers to the morass created by their "radical" social experimentation.

Young lives and minds are too precious and fragile to be toyed with by people who embrace some anti-American and anti-Christian agenda. Kids are bombarded with confusing messages; that a crucifix in urine, feces on a religious icon, and an American flag in a toilet are acceptable and protected, but public prayer is a crime. Or that animal life is sacred, but human life is expendable for the sake of convenience.

Or that burning the flag is protected speech, but desecrating the AIDS quilt is considered a "hate crime." Patriotism is diminished and Christianity is viewed as evil while consequences resulting largely from bad behavioral choices are viewed as noble and celebratory.

The politically correct practice of ignoring self-defeating behavior and refusing to urge youth to seek excellence only exacerbates the problem. Teen pregnancy is blamed on insufficient education about birth control methods rather than as a moral consequence of ignoring God's commands. Violent students who wreak havoc at school are often given victim status (they were ridiculed by others or bullied) when other students actually fear and avoid them.

We have surrendered our kids' minds to vulgar rappers, losers depicted as heroes, and TV and movie producers who glamorize everything from smoking and drug use to murder and satanic worship, without accepting any blame, whatsoever, for leading our youth astray.

Many leaders and "experts" moan that we have lost the war on drugs; therefore, we should legalize heroin, cocaine, marijuana, amphetamines, etc. They apparently believe that, instead of holding people liable for anti-social, destructive behavior, we can solve the problem by making the activity legal.

Many "surrender gurus," such as Dr. Dean Edell, believe hard drugs are no more dangerous than caffeine, liquor, or cigarettes. Never mind the terrible toll illegal drugs continue to take upon society. Others offer alcohol as proof that drugs can be legalized, regulated, and taxed, as if these steps would resolve the problems. One only needs to look at the deaths and injuries and families destroyed by drunk driving, drunken brawls, and crimes while under the influence to realize that such thinking is dangerously faulty.

Alcohol has caused its own share of social destruction, so it cannot be seriously offered as justification for legalizing hard drugs. But, the addiction levels are hugely disparate. Rarely do people commit capital crime for a drink, but drug addicts frequently kill for their next fix. Mothers sell their infants for drugs, but not for a drink. Instead of surrendering, we as a nation should be standing firm by teaching our young to strive for the best and avoid counter-productive, dangerous choices. In Proverbs 4, we are told to "Take hold of instruction, do not let go. Keep her, for she is your life. Do not enter the path of the wicked. Avoid it." The consequences of disobedience to God's law serve both to chastise the guilty and warn others who may be considering such activity. Removing consequences leads to destruction of the person you intend to protect. Now is not the time for surrender.

CORE VALUES ARE THE KEY
TO A SATISFYING LIFE

During a public forum on ethics and morality, one panelist stated that he believed that morality is something that is defined by each individual, based upon his frame of reference. He opined that one person's moral view may differ from that of another.

His question was, how do you know whose view of morality is correct? Another believed that, in this age of moral relativity, truth is subjective and changeable and each person gets to define his or her own version of truth.

I stated that the best way to avoid such confusion about truth and morality is to first find and embrace indisputable truth and a moral code of values. Then all of one's opinions and positions on issues will be viewed within the framework of that known truth and conviction. Finally, purpose not to compromise in those areas.

I was asked how to find "truth" and "core values." Core values are the basis for making life decisions and are established in conviction and integrity. Core values are interwoven into your person and do not change when you are tempted to violate those convictions for the sake of convenience.

For instance, I have a core value against stealing; therefore, I don't have to decide whether or not to take something that is not mine, even if there is no chance of getting caught. When one has embraced the truth, as set forth in Scripture, and specifically God's Ten Commandments, and is determined not to violate those Commandments, blessings come.

A person with no core conviction will base actions upon opportunity rather than on morality. I have a core conviction against taking illegal drugs or committing crime; therefore, there would be no struggle when faced with temptation to do either. I have taken a conscious, principled stand against committing crime, doing drugs, lying, etc.

A core set of values means that you steadfastly adhere to a code of conduct and principles by which you order your life. When pressured to operate outside of that code, a core set of values will likely keep you from making such a mistake. The lie of moral relativity insists that there are many versions of the truth, and that is a clear deception. The Bible tells us in 2 Cor. 10, that we should, "... take every thought captive to make it obedient to Christ..." By doing this, we fortify ourselves against blindly following people, programs or philosophical concepts that oppose our strongly held beliefs.

Compromise is often necessary in life, but not when it requires you to abandon moral values or personal integrity. It is said that if you don't stand for something, you will fall for anything. A person who depends upon others to define his position on issues or societal trends, may not have core values.

Don't compromise, don't be wishy-washy, supporting one side of an issue today, another tomorrow. Be consistent.

Give your children a road map that will serve them well as they navigate the often treacherous path through life. That road map and compass are the Holy Scriptures.

Embrace a core set of values for your life and teach your children values and ethics. The Ten Commandments are viewed by some as outdated and not applicable to today's lifestyles and morals. Not true. God's Word is essential to ordering one's life today. The Scriptures are eternally true, and are indispensable in embracing and teaching core values.

In answer to the question as to whose moral values one should embrace; there is only one truth, one moral code that brings about happiness. The Lord wants us to embrace His truth only, and not follow our failed human hearts. He warns us in Psalms 6, "… keep your father's commands and do not forsake your mother's teachings. Bind them upon your heart forever; fasten them around your neck. When you walk, they will guide you; when you awake, they will speak to you."

When we fail to meet His standards, God wants us to turn to Him in prayer and repentance for our sins. Through Christ, He forgives, undeservedly, and leads us to abundant life on earth and eternal life with Him.

NO HEAVEN OR HELL? I WOULDN'T BET ON IT!

We humans struggle with the "mystery" of life after death. Many people believe they have had a "near-death" experience. Others believe they actually died, but were sent back from Heaven to continue life on earth. I've never heard a report of anyone going to Hell and being sent back. Hmm.

I would never challenge another person's belief that he or she experienced an after-life phenomena. I, myself, experienced something that probably could be construed as a near-death experience, but that's a story for another time.

A famous Beatles song begins, "Imagine there's no Heaven … it's easy if you try. No Hell below us … above us … only sky." Imagine, indeed. It's not really as easy as John Lennon tried to make it sound. The Beatles earned lots of money with that song, and at the same time, probably sowed seeds of doubt in the hearts of many.

John Lennon and George Harrison have now gone on to discover the realities of all realities. If the theme of their song was true, then they flowed into nothingness when they died.

If the song's premise was wrong (as it most certainly was), then few would trade places with them now. I don't mean to pick on The Beatles. It is totally acceptable in today's society to reject biblical teachings and lean upon weak, failed human intellect, but one does so at his own peril.

Atheists believe they can destroy Christianity be removing its symbols, such as the Ten Commandments or a nativity scene, from their presence. The Bible tells us in Psalms, "…The fool says in his heart, 'There is no God.'" People who reject the possibility of a living God who created us and all there is, are perfectly willing accept the idea that a loud bang, created out of nothing, resulted in all that exists in the Universe.

Still others believe themselves to be too intelligent to believe in or depend upon anything or anyone other than themselves. They express that believing in God is only a silly crutch used by the weak to gain substance in their lives, since they have little or no control of their destiny. Many in this group believe that by eating the right foods, protecting their "Mother Earth," and helping social causes, they can live forever, and never be held to account for sins in their lives. The Bible tells us that we are to be good stewards of the earth and its assets, but not to worship them. It also tells us that we have no real control of any facet of our lives.

The Bible clearly expresses the existence of both Heaven and hell. Jesus gives a parable about a rich man who died and was buried and in hell, being in torment. He cried out for mercy, and for Lazarus to come and, "…Dip the end of his finger in water and cool my tongue; for I am in anguish in this flame."

God's word tells us that we are all sinners, and payment for our sin is death. Jesus Christ died and paid the price for our sin, then rose from the dead. He offers eternal life to all who receive His precious gift.

A person once stated that he couldn't believe that God could condemn to hell those in remote areas and have no chance to hear His word. But, Romans 1 tells us, "For what can be known about God is plain to them, because God has shown it to them." Ever since the creation of the world his invisible nature, namely, his eternal power and deity, has been clearly perceived in the things that have been made. So they are without excuse.

So, to paraphrase common law, ignorance of the "Lord" is no excuse.

WAS CAIN A VICTIM OF CHEMICAL IMBALANCE?

Political correctness tells us that everyone is a victim of someone or something else, and thereby, not responsible for his choices, decisions or actions. A group of political correctness intellectuals tell us that crimes such as rape, murder, and robbery are not the willful manifestation of bad choices, greed, selfishness or evil intent, but may actually be caused by air and water pollution.

According to the group, Detroiters Working for Environmental Justice, crime is most prevalent in the big cities of America due, in part, to lead paint often found in old houses. Further, many factories located in cities discharge chemicals such as manganese into the air. The conclusion is then drawn that brain damage, leading to criminal activity, is probably caused by that environment.

They believe biological factors cause people to lose control of their impulses because lead and other chemicals, "…alter human brain chemistry and eventually lower victims' self control." To these "pioneers," biochemistry is the basis of human behavior, and children who live near factories and in older homes are disproportionately exposed to chemicals. Poisons ingested from these chemicals lead them to participate in crime. They further surmise, even in absence of any evidence, since lead poisoning has been linked to hyperactivity and learning disabilities, that it is also a major cause of aggression.

Let's suppose that PC had been around at the time of Adam and Eve. Cain would have been labeled a victim, for sure. After all, his mother spent time listening to some serpent. His father joined her in bad choices, resulting in eviction from a perfect home. The family had to toil in the soil every day, exposing poor Cain to dangerous chemicals such as lead and manganese.

Food had to be cooked over an open fire, exposing the kids to smoke and carcinogens. Cain felt abandoned by his dysfunctional family and by God. The overwhelming effect of the chemicals to which he had been exposed (through no fault of his own) caused him to become aggressive and kill his brother (who, incidentally, had been exposed to the same elements and family situation with no such ill effects).

Our "experts'" excuses for criminal activity are just as ridiculous as the above scenario. In order to accept this newest theory, there are a few clearly visible factors that must be ignored, such as the fact that many children who turn to crime live in one-parent homes, and/or receive little or no direction or supervision. And that they are daily bombarded, not by chemicals, but with the electrical impulses and visual stimuli from movies and music that is negative, immoral, and destructive. A social environment that lacks positive role models is much more deadly than an environment filled with chemicals and lead paint.

Criminal activity is more likely spawned, in part, by

the lack of leadership within inner city communities. Many community leaders are more interested in furthering their agenda (which usually enriches the leader rather than assisting the poor), than really changing lives.

The main cause of criminal activity is that people make the wrong choices. Since violent crime takes place where factories and old houses don't exist, such as Columbine, and Paducha, and is committed by those who haven't been exposed to lead or factory waste, this "study" is easily refuted as baseless.

The Bible tells us that we are all sinners, and that out of man's heart comes all manner of evil. The focus should be on turning young hearts back to God by teaching them to obey everything Christ taught us, and teaching them to ask God to create in them a clean heart. Blaming chemicals for what comes from the heart is simply a dangerous smokescreen.

ASHAMED OF BEING
A CHRISTIAN?

I t becomes clearer each day that Satan is very busy trying to hold back the work of the Christian church. Many people in the media and leading social personalities have succeeded in demonizing Christianity, speaking of "the Christian Right" with disdain, as though being a Christian is something to be ashamed of. Many in the media gleefully report each and every human failing within the church. As a result, many Christians are ashamed of being easily identified as such.

Even Christ's disciples, at times, were ashamed or afraid of being exposed as Christians. Peter even denied Christ three times. And the world believes that if it can stifle even the mention of God's or Christ's name, it will somehow cause Christ and His church to cease to exist. But Christ tells us in His Word that if we remained silent, the very rocks and stones would testify that He is the Savior of the world.

Christ warns us that if we are ashamed of Him before mankind, He will be ashamed of us before His Father. Christians are asked to be prepared to declare Christ as Savior and Lord, even in the face of death. That's a heavy responsibility, but it is nothing when compared to what He has done for us.

An elderly pastor who had suffered persecution in prison for many years in the former Soviet Union once told a story about an underground church service that was interrupted by armed men who burst in, loudly demanding that all Christians stand up and move to one side of the room. They then commanded all of the others to leave, as the Christian believers prepared to die. The "attackers" then told the believers to relax. They were also believers, but, before they joined the group, they had to weed out the deceptive non-believers in their midst. The group could then worship in earnest.

This same pastor made it through the persecution by holding onto the truth that man can destroy the body, but cannot harm one's soul. The moving hymn "It is Well With My Soul" became his theme song throughout his captivity and afterward.

When traveling in foreign countries, I have often found myself in an area inhabited by groups that are antagonistic to Christians. I have played a scenario over in my mind during which I am confronted and asked whether I am a Christian. I believe that the Lord would have me answer in the affirmative, even in the face of harm or death. It would be a true test of my faith, but I believe that the Lord would deliver me, one way or the other.

However, I cannot even take credit for the faith, courage, and whatever else gives me the peace to be ready to declare my love for the Lord in any circumstance. He gives me the faith to believe and the courage to stand strong on those beliefs. Who couldn't trust a Savior like that?

I once was afraid to pray out loud in a group. I told

myself that prayer is such a personal time with the Lord, that it might be construed by others as boasting if I prayed out loud. Through growth in my walk with Christ, I now know that He wants me to lead others, particularly my family, in prayer. He gives me the words to say, and by praying, I am teaching my family valuable life lessons, such as being bold in declaring Christ as Lord, and thanking Him for our blessings.

Not every Christian feels led to stand on a street corner with a megaphone, shouting Scripture verses and calling others to repentance, but we are called to express and share our faith with others, and to proudly display Scripture references in our homes and wherever we go.

Hanging in a high and visible place in my home is a plaque, reflecting a verse from Joshua, "As for me and my house, we will serve the Lord." Anyone who enters will have no problem identifying that we are, indeed, a Christian family. Ashamed? Absolutely not! We are proud to have been picked as heirs by the King of all Kings.

A FATHER'S DAY LEGACY

The media is preoccupied with each president's efforts to build a legacy during the last months of his presidential tenure. Is a legacy created through one's concerted effort, or does it arise from whom that person was and what he stood for in terms of such attributes as decency, integrity and honesty? A true legacy leads others to pattern their lives after you—the real you—not who you packaged yourself to be.

I prefer rather to reflect upon the fact that I was blessed with the legacy of not one, but two fathers, neither of whom tried to build a legacy, but who both had a very significant impact on my life. Although my birth father, Samuel Jackson, died when I was three years old, he left me the only true legacy he was able to leave—his reputation.

Samuel Jackson, his four brothers, and one sister were born to Mississippi sharecroppers. They were reared to be respectful, hard-working, God-fearing, and patriotic. Slavery had ended less than fifty years before Samuel was born, and the last remnants of that era died hard. The family had to learn to be diplomatic and tactful in the cruel Jim Crow South, where a simple misunderstanding could result in a lynching.

This family was respected and well liked by virtually everyone they encountered. By adulthood, Sam was known as "good man." His brother, David, was called "solid," both because of his six-foot five chiseled frame and his dependable, helpful, consistent nature. When Sam died from a brain tumor in 1952, many of his friends thought "good man" was his real name, because it so accurately described his personality and love for others.

On his deathbed, Sam asked David to help our mother care for us. When she died just one year later, David, who only had one child of his own, took all ten of us into his home. David, or "Uncle Solly," as we called him, demonstrated strong moral character and taught us to work hard, be honest, and respect others.

He always reminded us of who we are and from whom we came. He kept our parents alive by telling us of their personal integrity and their love for us. Everyone who had known my father gave the same description of him. We had no doubt that he was, indeed, a good man who loved others unconditionally.

My uncle's approach to life reflected my father's character. He taught us lessons like "respect is not something one demands, but something one earns." We learned to look others in the eye and offer a firm handshake because David believed that the eyes and handshake say a lot about a person.

He taught us that God loved us, and even though He had taken our parents from us, He still had a plan for each of our lives. He taught us that skin color mattered little in the final analysis, and that no one can take away from you the good things that you choose to make a part of your life. When many blacks replaced their surnames with "X," he taught me that my name is not a "slave name." It was the proud name of many of my forebears; therefore, it is more important that I never discredit or shame my name than to dwell on how I got that name.

He taught me that, whether signing a check or a document, making a promise, or taking an oath, my name is the representation of who I am. If I use my name to lie, cheat, and or steal, then my name becomes, "liar," "cheater," or "thief."

I came to realize that if I live my life in a way that is pleasing to the Lord, I will be known as "good man" here on earth, and "good and faithful servant" by God one day. As he lay dying from a stroke, David reminded me that I still have a father who will "never leave me or forsake me."

Because of my two fathers, the legacy I desire to leave to my children, grandchildren, family, and friends is, "here was a good man." Next to that, everything else I may accomplish has little significance.

SCHOOL SHOOTINGS RAISE
SERIOUS QUESTIONS

Of the four school shootings in recent weeks, the most heart-rending was the slaughter of five Amish girls in their one-room Pennsylvania school house. But, all of the shootings are just as tragic, because they illustrate a danger-ous, growing trend of violence among our youth, in and out of school.

We all ponder the causes of such senseless loss of life. The usual justifications are offered: He was abused as a child, bullied at school, improperly potty trained, etc. A White House conference on school safety was convened to tackle the problem, but it is doubtful that any workable solution will arise from the conference.

Society's attempts to resolve violence such as school shootings, robberies, and murder among our young are doomed to failure because our "rules of engagement" are flawed. Political correctness prohibits seeking a morality-based solution; therefore we often completely ignore the spiritual aspect of the problem. We can't tell parents that God holds them responsible for instilling His word in their children. We aren't even allowed to consider pure evil as a cause.

By distorting our founders' efforts to keep government out of our religious life, social engineers prohibit moral teachings in schools, resulting in a twisted "freedom from religion." Instead of using Christian principles to provide a moral compass, morality is considered a threat to children. Political correctness tells children that no matter what they do or become, it is someone else's fault. Posting the Ten Commandments is treated as a terrorist act.

The killer of the Amish students reportedly called his wife and told her, in part, that he hated God and hated himself. Conversely, he asked the young girls to pray for him. It was reported that he told his wife that he felt extremely lonely. Could it have been a "God-shaped hole" in his heart that the Lord yearned to fill? He had hugged and kissed his own children goodbye as he placed them on their school bus, shortly before entering the one-room school and wreaking havoc upon the lives of so many.

How can such love and such hatred reside simultaneously in one heart? His claim that he sexually abused two relatives when he was twelve was disputed by the "victims." Was his young mind allowed to cultivate and dwell upon evil acts? Did he carry real or imagined lust with him into adulthood without any person reaching out to him with words or actions to re-direct him toward moral living?

The shooter at another school wore a long black trench coat, as did the suicidal kids at Columbine High School. The black trench coat is symbolic of satanic-laced beliefs, such as Wicca and Goth, to which numerous children subscribe, and which are allowed in school. Could tolerance for any religion except Christianity be an element in the increasing violence we are seeing today?

Young people are slipping into dangerous, deadly lifestyle choices, while parents and others look the other way, until their dangerous secrets erupt in unimaginable ways. These youth often know nothing of a loving God who created them and set rules for their lives, rules that would likely lead to a happy full life, rather than one of total despair.

Could a steady diet of immoral TV shows and movies have dulled their senses to the needs of others, resulting in a totally selfish state of mind that honors neither life nor property? Could the cheapening of life that has resulted in millions of abortions have leeched into their minds and lessened the value of all life?

Could daily exposure to the Commandments have reminded them that God says, "Love one another," and "Thou shalt not murder"? Perhaps the Amish school shooting would not have occurred if the shooter had been taught the blessed concept of forgiveness that the Amish community offered so freely to him after his contemptible actions.

There may be more questions than answers. It's so sad youth aren't taught where to look for the answers.

WHAT IS COMMITMENT?

The concept of commitment has been victimized by today's extreme focus upon self. Loyalty and dedication are considered undesirable or even laughable traits. Commitment in marriage, family, child rearing, business or politics is considered antiquated and inessential by current cultural dictates.

Pre-nuptial agreements were mostly unheard of years ago. Today, most advisors encourage such agreements to protect each partner's rights to money, children, and possessions. Had I suggested a prenuptial when I proposed to my wife, she probably would have suggested we enter into a "no nuptial" agreement, and go our separate ways. Marriage was ordained as an institution that should be approached reverently, spiritually, and permanently. When initiated within the proper spirit, a man and woman can enter into the "free fall" of committed love. Trust is essential in marriage; the kind of trust shown in a reliance-building game in which one partner falls backward and trusts the other person to catch him or her. Today's TV talk shows would rather the person allow their mate to collapse to the floor for the humor of it. It's all about trust. A pre-nuptial agreement doesn't reflect true trust and commitment. In fact, it illustrates just the opposite-mistrust and selfishness.

Many people enter into marriage with little or no commitment, focusing only upon themselves. Marriage is a covenant, instituted by God, which should be enjoined only after prayerful meditation. Mark 10:7–8 says, "For this reason a man shall leave his father and mother and be joined to his wife, and the two shall become one flesh, so then they are no longer two, but one flesh." Society tells us that each partner should remain an individual. One young couple who insisted upon a church wedding expressed that their commitment was based upon a "12–24 check," whereby they would check after one year, and again after two years to determine whether they really loved one another. If not, the marriage would end. The marriage lasted less than two years. With such lack of loyalty, failure was a foregone conclusion.

The appalling divorce rate could be greatly decreased if people would, first of all choose a mate who shares their values, who shares the same belief system, and is willing to rear children in the fear and admonition of the Lord. Some of the new practices often included in weddings today make a mockery of the love that should emanate from marriage, such as the bride and groom smashing wedding cake into each other's face. Commitment means making a "bottom line" pledge to each other that every situation, disagreement, major decision, problem, will be handled in the framework that their love for one another is the bottom line, and that no circumstance could change that. When commitment is foremost in marriage, child rearing or any sort of partnership, the probability of success is greatly enhanced. But commitment is the one ingredient lacking in so many relationships.

For example, too many parents neglect the covenant

between themselves and their children. God gives specific and frequent direction to discipline children in love, and to train, guide, and protect them from harm. Especially, we are commanded to bring them to a knowledge of the Lord. Today, people abuse, neglect, and harm children, in spite of Christ's dire warning, "It would be better for him if a millstone were hung around his neck, and he were thrown into the sea, than that he should offend one of these little ones" (Luke 17:2; Matt. 18:6; Mark 9:42). Apparently, many do not realize the consequences of disobeying the Lord. Many parents allow children to make dangerous decisions and call the shots in situations where the child cannot possible have the information or cognizance to make correct choices.

God also expects us to be committed when we take on a job, enter a partnership, sign an agreement, take an oath (for we are swearing before God), or promise to do something. He wants us to show the greatest measure of commitment by fulfilling His Great Commission by making disciples for Christ, and teaching them obedience to all that He has taught us. We must be committed enough to approach every relationship and every task from His perspective. His call to commitment is fulfilled when others see Christ in us.

RE-SEGREGATION AND OTHER
SELF-INFLICTED INJURIES

A study reports an alarming movement back to re-segregating the races. The separation of the races seems to be most evident in the nation's schools. It states that, if the trend continues, blacks face extreme reductions and reversals of gains since the Civil Rights laws were enacted.

The study seemed to insinuate that schools are re-segregating, because of a return to Jim Crow laws. Not true. Some folks transfer their children from schools with mixed-race populations for reasons of safety. It is easy to label parents as racists when they only desire to relocate their students to a more productive, safe environment.

Few parents want to see their kids trapped in the failed armed camps called public schools, but what alternative is there? Politicians, teachers, black leaders, and affluent whites who send their kids to out-of-district or private schools often are the same elitists who keep blacks from following suit by vehemently opposing vouchers for school choice.

Most predominately black charter schools are Muslim-oriented. It is not racism to refuse to send your child to a school which is based upon a religion that you do not practice. Also, a visit to any public school will show you who displays the most bigotry and who is initiating segregation. Sadly, it is usually black students. Rural schools are mostly white because few blacks desire to live in those communities.

Black leaders must make efforts to reduce the over-involvement of young black kids in crime and self-destructive behavior and increase the numbers of black kids who excel academically. Young blacks are allowed to have a "black prom," which further divides people socially. It would be ignorant to infer that bias and prejudice do not exist. Sadly, as long as human nature persists, we will always divide each other along lines of differences, while espousing a coming together and a celebration of differences.

All people need to be taught, from early childhood throughout life, that there are good and bad people of every race. Dr. Martin Luther King, Jr., implored us to begin judging people by the content of their character rather than the color of their skin. Jesus Christ gave us a new Commandment that includes all of the others, "Love one another." Love others because the Lord said so, and because, to do so fills the spaces in our hearts with something that heals and inspires, leaving little or no room for hatred and bias.

If we allow kids to segregate from each other, when will they learn to live and work with others who are not like them? When they enter the working world, college, or the military, they will carry with them either the hatred and the habits they formed of looking for differences, or God's love, which allows them to see others as brothers and sisters.

Loving one another is not a practice, something you consciously do each time you meet another. It is a mindset and a heart-set whereby you decide that, as a part of your

make-up, you will seek to show the love of Christ to everyone you encounter, through your countenance, and through
your actions. When this becomes a part of you, you lose the
desire to separate, and you desire to serve others, which is the
evidence of love.

SCOTTY WOLFE
MOCKS NO MORE

The headlines sadly announced that the man who held the world's record for the most legal marriages had died just ten days before his one-year wedding anniversary. Someone opined that "Scotty" Wolfe, who had been married twenty-nine times, would be very bored in his next life, since he had "done it all" in this life. The newspaper article explained that Scotty never really got that part about "till death do us part." They sadly reported that, after two weeks, no one had come to claim Scotty's corpse.

Scotty's grieving widow lived hundreds of miles away, and couldn't afford to bury him, or even attend any service for him. Wolfe was eventually cremated, and his remains were interred in an unmarked "Potter's field" outside Los Angeles, California. His son explained his father's multiple marriages, stating that his dad, " ... married so often because he was against living in sin. He was also picky and stubborn." Apparently old Scotty divorced one wife for eating sunflower seeds in bed, and another for using his tooth brush.

Scotty's son, John, isn't sure whether his dad really

fathered the nineteen children ascribed to him, or whether he really had forty grandchildren and nineteen great grandchildren. John has never met any of them. In fact, John never met his own mother, wife number fourteen. But, John proudly expresses that his Guinness Book of Records title holder father had, for more than thirty-five years, been a "Bible-thumping minister." By the way, his latest wife had, herself, been married twenty-three times.

It is amazing that a man who professes to be a minister would live a life that is such a mockery to everything he supposedly stands for. Society gives a collective shrug and a wink at behavior that is truly disgusting, as well as blasphemous. We readily elevate people like Wolfe to celebrity status, when they should be shunned, castigated, and rebuked for their actions.

I think the information that Wolfe was a minister for thirty-five years struck me as hard as his vast number of marriages. God designed marriage for one man and one woman—for life. Because of our sin condition, we make mistakes that lead to divorce, and many repent and ask God for and receive forgiveness and live changed lives. But, even though divorce seems to be endemic in today's society, twenty-nine nuptials is still way beyond the pale.

A person married twenty-nine times is operating more from a bad habit than from any belief in the sanctity of marriage. In Hebrews, God says that marriage "…is honorable among all, and the bed undefiled, but fornicators and adulterers God will judge." As a "Bible-thumping" minister, Wolfe was a held to a higher standard. In 2 Peter 2, we are warned of "…false prophets and teachers, who bring in destructive heresies, even denying the lord who bought them, and bring upon themselves swift destruction." By his lifestyle, Scotty Wolfe confirmed that he fit this description.

So, it is safe to assume that the late Mr. Wolfe is not somewhere in suspended animation contemplating what he will do in the next life. God also says in Hebrews, "And it is appointed for man to die once, but after this the judgment." Since we don't know Mr. Wolfe's heart, we don't know whether he repented and received the free gift of eternal life through Jesus Christ, but we do know that, according to the Bible, he isn't coming back to this life in any form.

Mr. Wolfe's lifestyle clearly mocked God and His Word. He clearly led others astray as a minister who demonstrated such contempt for the sacred Commandments of God. It's safe to assume that, whether or not he had a deathbed conversion, he mocks God no more!

THE TELL-TALE HEART IN
THE NEW MILLENNIUM?

When I was a child, I was intrigued and chilled by Edgar Allan Poe's shocking tale, "The Tell-tale Heart." The story is told by a narrator who goes to great lengths to assure the reader that he is not crazy.

He takes his time in relating how much he loved his dear, old friend, but that the friend had a pale, blue eye, "Like that of a vulture," that haunted the narrator. Each night he would go in and shine a light on the eye, only to be repelled in revulsion. On the eighth night of this ritual, he smothered the old man and placed his body beneath the floor boards.

The police arrived in response to neighbors' reports of screams coming from the house, but the narrator calmly convinced the police that nothing had happened there. But as he conversed with the police, he began hearing the old man's heart beating, first softly, then louder, louder, louder. He couldn't understand why the police couldn't hear the beating. When he could take no more, he screamed his confession. He had killed the man. Could O.J. Simpson be in the throes of a Tell-tale Heart syndrome?

Just as the public at large was beginning to accept the saga of former football star, O.J. Simpson's dramatic trial and acquittal of the murders of his former wife and her friend, Ron Goldman, as just another unsolvable crime, O.J., himself, has brought it back to the fore.

He has written a book which proposes that, if he had committed the grizzly crime, how he would have done it! He has begun offering interviews to anyone who is interested to tell the world how he would have murdered two people—if he had done so. One former detective on the original case explains that O.J.'s description of how he would have committed the crime closely parallels the way the crime was really perpetrated.

John 3:20 tells us, "Everyone who does evil hates the light, and will not come into the light for fear that his deeds will be exposed." But, we were also created with a conscience, which knows and reminds us of every thought, word, and deed that we perform. I believe that particularly hideous acts reside in the forefront of our conscience and may torment us constantly.

People quite often speak of a "perfect crime." First of all, this is an oxymoron, since crime cannot be perfect. There are sometimes crimes, even murder, that go undetected or unsolved for many years, but who knows the torment the perpetrator suffers. They may not hear the victim's heart pounding in their ears, but many researchers believe that the heartbeat that tortured the narrator was his own heart, which could not contain the evil deed he had done.

O.J. still insists that he is innocent of the murders. He has, by all human standards, "beat the rap." He was found responsible for the deaths in a civil trial, and owes the victims' families thirty-three million dollars, that he avoided by claiming poverty. But, he cannot be tried again for the murders because of double jeopardy laws. He lives a carefree life of golf, travel, and fun. So, why would he bring the whole sordid mess up again, especially in a manner in which he seems to be pointing his own guilty finger at himself?

We may never know, but God knows, and He says, "Your sin will find you out."

THANK HIM, ANYWAY

While standing in line at a customer service desk, I overheard someone say, "Thanksgiving? I don't have anything to be thankful for!" The speaker and another person then launched into what seemed to be a competition to see who could come up with the saddest tale of woe. I thought how sad it was that these people could think of nothing for which to be thankful.

It brought to mind the many family Thanksgiving dinners I experienced as a child, and those my immediate family have experienced. I come from a family of ten siblings, and many cousins, aunts and uncles, and extended family members. We had large food feasts on Thanksgiving, and established certain customs and ground rules.

Everyone was admonished to dwell upon the good things in life, and anyone who brought up a negative topic was castigated by the group. Before we sat down to dinner, we stood and held hands around the long table, and each person (except for those too young to speak), had to express thanks for at least one person or thing in their lives. Anyone who couldn't think of anything be thankful for could expect a session of one-on-one counseling with my Aunt Bessie later in the day.

Sometimes, by the time we went all the way around the table, and my Uncle Dave finished his long Thanksgiving prayer and blessing, I worried that the food would get cold before we ate (it never did). I carried this custom on after I had a family of my own. We also had a custom of inviting a person or family who would otherwise spend Thanksgiving alone, to join our family for dinner. I continued this custom, and throughout the years, we have enjoyed the company of many interesting people, including a student from Africa and his family who spoke only Swahili; a college basketball player; a homeless person that my young daughter suggested we invite, and others.

Many who tend to dwell upon all the things they don't have, or on their problems often ignore the many blessings they have experienced in life. One person may dwell upon a broken relationship between her and her child, while forgetting the blessing of healing from cancer that she, herself, received. One person might dwell upon the loss of a job, while neglecting to give thanks for having the good health to seek another one. Another might dwell upon having failed to obtain the new car he desires, rather than giving thanks for dependable transportation.

I remember my Aunt Bessie responding to a family member who stated that he could find nothing for which to give thanks, "You woke up this morning, didn't you? You're standing there breathing, aren't you? Then, thanks be to God for that! If you don't feel particularly thankful, thank Him anyway!"

God doesn't promise us perfect health and happiness, or wealth and prosperity. Instead, He warns us in His word that we will have trials and tribulation. In 1 Thessalonians, He tells us to "…Give thanks in all circumstances, for this is God's will for you in Christ Jesus." He also tells us in Phil. 6, "Do not be anxious about anything, but in everything, by prayer and petition, with thanksgiving, present your requests to God."

Therefore, even if it is true that you cannot think of one thing for which to give thanks, God wants you to thank him for the struggles and bad things, asking Him to deliver you from them. So, Happy Thanksgiving, and if you can't think of anything to give thanks for, thank God anyway.

WHO WANTS TO LIVE FOREVER?

The new wave of TV game shows range from the interesting "Who Wants to be a Millionaire?" to "Greed" to the mockery of the covenant of marriage called, "Who Wants To Marry A Multimillionaire?" which, thankfully, was quickly exposed as a huge fraud. Let's pretend there is game show "Who Wants to Live Forever?" in which everyone is eligible to play. The prize—eternal life.

The game consists of one question with one correct answer and trillions of wrong ones. The contest has three lifelines, as follows:

1. 50/50, where, instead of two incorrect answers being removed, trillions of wrong answers disappear, leaving only the correct answer.

2. Instead of polling the audience, the contestant can get the answer from a one-in-three person panel that always gives the correct answer.

3. The contestant may call on someone who may know the answer, except, in this game, the person on the other end

of the phone fully knows the answer, and is waiting patiently for the contestant to call ask for help.

The contestant, as on the other game shows, may rant and rave, pondering one answer after another, heading off in one direction, then another, in search of the elusive answer to the question. The answer is actually right in front of the contestant's nose, but seems to be all too simple. Even after using all of his lifelines, he is still uncertain of the correct answer. He fears that choosing what appears to be the obvious may cause him to lose out on a loftier prize that waits just over the next hill.

The contestant murmurs to himself, "I've always believed that anything that seems to be too good to be true, probably is, and that anything that is gained outside of my own efforts is probably not worth having. Throughout my life, I have been able to operate well by measuring the benefits and risks, and then making a decision based upon my wisdom and my best guess. This situation is requiring me to make a decision relying on something outside myself, trusting on someone else's promise."

The contestant's human nature tells him not to trust his lifelines. He believes they may have the answer, but he is not quite ready to place such a monumental decision in someone else's hands just yet. A light suddenly shines on an empty chair next to him, and something tells him that the chair obviously looks like it is capable of holding his weight, should he sit in it. But the chair isn't doing a thing for him simply because he knows it is capable of holding him.

But, if he goes over and sits in the chair, he will be putting his faith in the chair to hold him. The contestant begins to understand the difference between belief and faith. Knowing the chair could hold him is one thing, but putting enough trust and faith in the chair to sit in it is another thing.

The contestant prays out loud to be rescued from this dilemma. The calm assurance comes quickly to his heart. He now understands that all of his wisdom and strength and cleverness fall woefully short of what is required to obtain the prize he seeks. He now knows that he cannot earn the prize through his own efforts. It is a free gift!

Thinking out loud, he declares that he now understands that believing that his lifelines can save him is one thing, but he must trust in them enough to risk everything by placing his all in those lifelines, and not upon his own understanding or ingenuity. Two Scripture verses from his youth enter into his mind; "There is a way that seems right to man, but in the end, it leads to death;" and "Trust in the Lord, and lean not upon your own understanding."

The answer to the quest for eternal life is not found in his own efforts because his sinful nature prohibits him from coming to God. Therefore, he has to trust in someone who is righteous and acceptable to God, who will stand in the gap between the contestant and God; a gap created by the contestant's own sin. That person is Jesus Christ; that Triune Lifeline is the Father, Son, and Holy Spirit. And that's the final answer!

HONOR THY FATHER
AND THY MODEM

Family courts have taken a giant step toward replacing old-fashioned parenting with modern technology. Courts believe the use of web cameras will "revolutionize" parental visitation. A New Jersey judge ordered a non-custodial father to buy a computer and web camera for himself and one for his nine-year-old daughter, who was about to move to California with her mother, so that the father and child could have "virtual visitation."

An appeals court upheld the order, stating that a combination of online visitation and face-to-face contact would be a "creative and innovative way" for the father and daughter to keep in contact. Norman Trusch, a divorce attorney, thinks this is an excellent tool for solving the custodial parent relocation problem that is so prevalent in today's mobile society. "If I have clients who want to move, I'd tell them to offer to buy a web camera and set that up."

In Philadelphia, at least one judge regularly includes online technology as part of custody and visitation arrangements. According to judge Robert Matthews, "It can be educational for the children, and brings the parents together." Somehow, togetherness via computer monitor screen seems to be somewhat of a stretch. The judge also opined, "It doesn't take the place of a hug, but it sure beats not being able to see your kids grow up."

Perhaps the child should place a notch mark at his or her height level on the wall, and periodically make new marks and then aim the web cam at the spot so that the non-custodial parent can see how much the child has grown. Not only does this concept not replace hugs, it can't replace sitting down to dinner together, watching the child play sports, or an arm around the shoulder of a child who has had a bad day. "Hey, Billy, can you come over to play?" "Naw, I'm having 'virtual' dinner with my dad tonight."

Since the TV is often the main proponent in rearing children today and kids often worship and honor TV characters, perhaps a parent who only appears on the tube will have more influence over the child than a live-in parent. Probably not. Perhaps the video-parent could have the child scan the room from time to time just to assure that no bombs or weapons are being made or stored there, since, quite often, the custodial parent is prohibited from entering a child's room.

Another technological wonder is the off-site house monitoring system. One such system, the Xamboo (pronounced zam-boo), is a system that can be accessed from any computer. One can greet latchkey kids when they get home from school, and be readily available if the child needs to speak with the parent. The system will advise if a window or door is opened, if someone is in the swimming pool, if an off-limits area is entered, or even if a car pulls into the driveway.

Once the system is revised to bandage small cuts, call an ambulance and argue with the children about where they want to go and with whom, eating their vegetables, etc., we may not need parents anymore. While technology can be effectively used to assist parents and to allow more access to non-custodial parent, it cannot replace the structure that God put in place: the parents. He intended for parents to rear their children together. Divorce doesn't relieve parents of the responsibility to be a physical presence in the lives of their children.

When God said in Malachi 4:6, "And he shall turn the heart of the fathers to the children, and the heart of the children to their fathers," I don't think this is quite what he had in mind.

WORRY ABOUT SOULS,
NOT GLOBAL WARMING

Mark Twain once said, "God created Man in his own image and Man, being a generous sort, returned the favor." Nowhere is this more evident than in the current global warming controversy.

In order to subscribe to the current belief that we are doomed because we have the audacity to use the earthly elements God provided in order to live, feed, heat, and cool ourselves, one must either ignore what God has said, or believe that He didn't know what He was doing when He created us and the world. One glaring difference between mankind and God is that God is consistent, where mankind constantly changes its mind. God said that He created the earth for mankind, and that we were to subdue it, care for it, and have dominion over it and all life-sources.

We humans, meanwhile, can't seem to make up our minds. In the April 28, 1975, issue of Newsweek magazine, climatologists warned of a coming ice age within thirty years from that time. As evidence, they cited a drop of half a degree in average ground temperature between 1945 and 1968.

They also believed that our use of fossil fuels would result in droughts, floods, dry spells, and long freezes. They forecast a severe drop in food output around the globe "perhaps only ten years from now" (by 1985). But there was no drop in food production by 1985, nor has there been any since. Some scientists offered solutions to avoid the new Ice Age, such as deliberately melting the Artic ice cap or covering it with black soot, diverting Artic rivers, etc.

Today, we are alerted that the ice cap is melting from "greenhouse gases," a result of our use of the internal combustion engine. So within thirty years, we have gone from the threat of freezing to death to the threat of burning up, both from the same root cause, which apparently is everything mankind uses in the pursuit of happiness.

Such agenda-driven people are careful not to let facts get in the way of their march to prove that mankind is a plague upon the earth. For instance, shortly after I left the Philippines after my first trip there, Mt. Pinatubo erupted, killing thousands and wiping out numerous towns and villages, and spewing many times more ash and pollution into the atmosphere than man has ever caused.

When hurricane Katrina struck Mississippi and Louisiana, many experts said that this was the beginning of the end, and that such storms would increase in number and intensity from then on. The following year, about three named storms struck the U.S., causing little or no damage. Seismic activity, earthquakes, volcano eruptions, storms, pestilence, etc. have plagued the earth since sin came into the world by Adam and Eve, and will be here until Christ returns.

God tells us to expect such things and not spend time and effort figuring out how we may have caused them. Jesus tells us in Matthew, "You will hear of wars and rumors of wars, but see to it that you are not alarmed. Such things must happen, but the end is still to come ... "

The earth may be in a warming trend, and may have been in a cooling trend in 1975. This may do more to prove intelligent design than global warming. God created the earth to last until He declares it as no longer necessary.

Many people cry for peace, meaning the absence of conflict. As long as we sinful humans exist in our present state, sustained peace will not occur. Christ also told us, "Nation will rise against nation, and kingdom against kingdom ... These are the beginning of birth pains."

Instead of wasting time blaming ourselves for such signs, we, who believe in God's son, Jesus Christ, and trust in only Him for salvation, should be using the remaining time available to us to share His love and gift of eternal life with others. Much of the self-hating rhetoric only serves as a distraction from concern for lost souls, which is the greatest problem we face.

WELCOME, MR. CHAOS, WE'VE BEEN EXPECTING YOU!

B aby Boomers are searching everywhere for answers as to why our kids are falling into the cesspool of declining morals and destructive behavior. Everywhere, that is, except in the mirror.

We blame inanimate objects or other people rather than admit that many parents, operating out of their own rebellious and hateful nature, have passed on to their children a legacy of violence and self-destruction. We refuse to consider that many of the activities and ideologies many of us embraced in our youth and in our adult lives significantly impact our children.

There is a saying, "What parents do in moderation, children will do in excess." So, if the parents live lives of excess, how far will the children go? Well, we certainly are taking excess to new and frightening heights. Look at some of the cause and effect between the lives of many Baby Boomers and their offspring.

The 60s ushered in free love, drug abuse, and hatred for rules and authority. In the 70s, abortion was legalized.

The effect is out of control promiscuity, rampant STDs, HIV, and kids killing over drugs, or just for the thrill of it. Abortion is now allowed even during the delivery process. When we teach our young that life has no value, life has no value. Surprise!

Welfare, a temporary safety net, became a hammock for the lazy and a power tool for advocacy groups. Fathers were replaced by cradle-to-grave government hand-outs. In their zest for power, welfare advocates destroyed personal integrity and initiative, creating a dependency that now has to be painfully rooted out.

Many black leaders in the 60s civil rights struggles are now "Poverty Pimps," who label anyone with personal integrity and self-sufficiency as a "sell out," while promoting poverty to assure a mass of poor "victims." Guilt-ridden foundations then loosen their purse strings, but the funds mostly go to the already wealthy "leaders." Many young people embrace the "victim" label to get something for nothing.

Baby Boomers carried the protest of the Vietnam War over to a vicious hatred for our nation, flag, and creed. Once in charge, they have socially engineered the military to a dangerous state of non-readiness. Many of our kids refuse military service. And we wonder why.

In rebellion against conformity and good grooming, teens in the 60s were long-haired and unkempt. Their kids now wear droopy pants, with piercings and tattoos on every part of their anatomy. Sixties music ridiculed fidelity and committed love ("If you can't be with the one you love; love the one you're with"). Today's youth laugh at faithfulness and view promiscuity as normal and healthy.

Most Boomers fought against all forms of authority, abandoned the Bible, and embraced gurus and druggies for truth and purpose in life. They prohibit proven disciplinary measures for failed "pop-psychology." The new definition of "family" includes everything from same sex couples to people and their pets to group marriages. They believe in symbolism (talking about issues) over substance (actually doing something about issues). Then we wonder why our kids show so little honor, honesty or critical thinking.

By their hatred for God and His Word, Boomers have bestowed upon their kids a confusing, twisted view of good and evil, leaving them vulnerable to Satanism, paganism and the worship of evil people like Charles Manson. Many kids today don't know what God says about life, death, or sin. And Boomers ask, "Why?"

God warns us about violating His principles and seeking false gods, "I will visit the iniquity of the fathers upon the children to the third and fourth generations of those who hate me." How can we be surprised that pandemonium exists? We refuse to live by and teach God's life principles. And chaos results. We should, instead exclaim, "Welcome, Mr. Chaos … we've been expecting you!"

VISION-IMPAIRED
LEADERSHIP

Have you ever felt like the child in the story, *The Emperor's New Clothes*? Has your heart ever nagged you to speak the truth when everyone else seems to be buying a blatant lie? As we enter a new century, the state of ethics and values in our culture is dreadful. It is considered unacceptable to take a principled stand against wrong, evil, or a hidden agenda. And, as a black American, I am more alarmed by the lack of moral character among those whom many call leaders.

People willingly follow those whose motives and actions contradict their stated beliefs. But, as in the story, many whisper in private what they dare not declare in public; that the "emperors" are unable to conceal their moral flaws, no matter what righteous finery they wear. Most of today's leaders are not clothed in righteousness, but are really wearing nothing of essence, and are only after the power and influence position brings. Few people have the nerve to declare this.

Too many black leaders view racism as a precious jewel by which to gain personal wealth and relevance. The decrease in the institutional racism of the Jim Crow days creates a great dilemma for today's leaders. They are largely relegated to defending guilty people, championing filth as art, and blaming destructive behavior on anyone but the culpable, as long as the person is black.

The fear of many blacks to speak out against phony, self serving leaders is causing the masses to live in a type of bondage worse, in many ways, than slavery. How can we remain silent as a "leader" calls his demands for special dispensation for a group of serially truant thugs (some who are third-year freshman), a "righteous cause"? A true leader would denounce the behavior and tell the kids to take their punishment and turn away from destructive behavior. He would also chastise them for promoting the negative stereotypical image of black on black crime.

He would teach them that such activity is unacceptable and indefensible, and would hold the violent kids up as an example to other young people of how not to act, and thereby encourage others to stay away from bad behavior. Bailing kids out of consequences is not the way to build godly character. The rush to erase consequences just because of skin color is racism in reverse. It destroys character, which can lead to the total destruction of the person it intends to protect.

One "national leader" is fighting for the release of the thirteen-year-old Pontiac, Michigan, boy who shot another black teen, lamenting that, " … they are after our children!" A true leader would insist the boy be given the proper sentence for the crime, then placed with youth authorities until age twenty-one, during which time he would be required to complete high school, learn a trade, and get counseling to cure dangerous tendencies. Failure to complete these requirements would result in his being placed in an adult prison to serve out the original sentence. The poor choices of issues by today's leaders clearly shows that they have lost any semblance of the moral authority required to lead.

Anyone who stands against such foolishness is labeled a bigot, and, if black, is labeled an Uncle Tom. This epitaph is more fitting these leaders who work to keep people in bondage, than for those who stand up for what is right in order to free people from mental and emotional slavery.

A leader has to be a teacher, not one who makes excuses for bad people. A true leader sees opportunities to correct behavioral problems, instead of seeing a bigot behind every tree. The Bible speaks harshly of leaders who teach contrary to God's principles. 1 Tim. 6:3–4 says, "If anyone teaches otherwise and does not consent to wholesome words of our Lord Jesus Christ, and to the doctrines which accord with godliness, he is proud, knowing nothing, but is obsessed with disputes and arguments over words, from which come envy, strife, reviling, evil suspicions. Useless wrangling of men of corrupt minds and destitute of the truth, who suppose that godliness is means of gain. From such withdraw yourself."

Do you recognize any of today's black leaders in that passage? Sadly, I do. They're the ones wearing the invisible garments.

WHAT IS THE KEY TO
AN ABUNDANT LIFE?

Many of today's philosophers and anthropologists believe they have discovered the four major keys to living an abundant life. These "keys" are being heralded in books, speeches, and even over the Internet. Many believe that whoever embraces these important keys will experience a highly fulfilled life and leave a wonderful legacy after their life ends.

The four keys are:

1. To live, not just by breathing, but experiencing and enjoying all the earth offers.
2. To love and be loved, leaving each person one meets happier in every way.
3. To learn, getting to know the earth and its inhabitants, animal, vegetable, mineral.
4. To leave a legacy, bequeathing something noteworthy and lasting to posterity.

The inclusion of these four keys, according to those who espouse this concept, is the true path to success and true joy. The keys are being widely disseminated as profound and life-changing steps toward solving all of life's problems. Many deep thinkers opine that these keys should be posted in every schoolroom and boardroom. They are already appearing unsolicited in email boxes around the world.

We humans are always seeking a new way; an untried formula for resolving man's inhumanity to his fellow man and bringing true meaning to life, as well as making some kind of sense of life after it has been lived. In our vain efforts to discover a better way, we disregard the truths and road map that have already been placed before us.

We reject the only real methods and rules for living an abundant life here on earth, and we constantly look for an easier way to find substance after life. We allow others to prohibit us from teaching truth to our children, or even posting those truths where our young may be exposed to them. We then create "warm and fuzzy" sounding platitudes in a vain attempt to replace those abandoned and despised truths ordained by God.

God gave us His Commandments as a road map for life. He begins by commanding us to "love Him with all our heart, soul, mind, and strength." He created us, so He knows that we do not have the capacity to love others unless we first love Him who made us. He tells us to "love our neighbor as ourselves," and to honor Him and each other by not stealing, killing, stealing, or desiring that which belongs to others.

Rather than embracing and teaching those Commandments to our young, mankind makes laws against exposing God's rules for life to all people. Success, in God's eyes, is measured by how well we love, obey, and honor Him, because, when we do that well, honoring and loving each other is an inherent by-product of that love of God. True joy comes from sharing the message of God's unconditional love to every person we encounter, and telling others about a God who loves them so much that He sacrificed His only Son to pay for their sins, and who offers them eternal life as a free gift.

God wants us to live and learn more about His love for us. He teaches us to read His word and to teach it to our young. He tells us to talk about His word day and night, and to post His word on our doorposts and everywhere else. It is our sinful nature that tells us we can find a better way.

When we place our trust in creative sayings of our own design, rather than in the awesome power of God's word, the results are confusion and frustration. When we strive to live lives in obedience to all that the Lord has taught us, we find true happiness. There is no man-made joy that can compare to the joy of witnessing the miracle of a person praying to receive the free gift of eternal life through Jesus Christ.

And what about our legacy? There is no legacy greater than having faithfully done the work of the Lord here on earth. There is no recognition that could ever compare to hearing the voice of God as one enters His heaven saying, "Well done, good and faithful servant!"

TAKING THE
BULLYING PLEDGE

Victimhood is fashionable today. Minority leaders package their followers as victims in order to extract money and power from corporations and government. Politicians whine about being mistreated and trampled upon by their opponents. Many perpetrators of school violence are now provided the excuse that being bullied by others led them to maim and kill.

Despite proof that students at Columbine were largely terrified and intimidated by the young men who killed fifteen people, it has now been widely accepted as fact that the killers were somehow bullied and mistreated by the student body, provoking them to build bombs and obtain weapons to take revenge.

Since Columbine, there has been an explosion of efforts to end bullying in schools. Surveys are conducted to determine who becomes a bully and why. Psychologists and other experts who analyze this phenomenon basically agree that both the victims and the bullies suffer from low self-esteem.

It may be more likely that the root cause of this and other problems among our young stem from a lack of foundation.

Could it be that many of the concepts and creeds that have been labeled as dangerous, thereby drummed out of our children's lives and schools were the anchoring, teaching tools that kept such violence at bay for so many years? Is the posting of the Ten Commandments really dangerous to children, or might they show kids that someone greater than them has said that they shall not kill others? A teacher can no longer recite, "Do unto others as you would have them do unto you," for fear of establishing a religion.

Many schools believe that establishing their own set of commandments will bring about the same results that were consistently achieved over the years by teaching children biblical concepts.

Many schools now begin the day by reciting the "Pledge Against Bullying." The dichotomy of this effort is that, in order for any pledge that is based upon how we treat each other to succeed, it must include many of the very tenets that are rejected in banning God's commands.

The pledge includes concepts such as honesty, not desiring or taking what belongs to others, being truthful, not hurting others, citizenship, tolerance and courage. Other versions include words such as compassion, respect, self-discipline, and trustworthiness.

All of these attributes are included in the Bible. In the minds of today's enlightened leaders, changing the order and words of the Commandments, and not attributing them to God, somehow makes them acceptable and non-threatening to the "freedom from religion" crowd.

The solemn truth is that, just as in grief counseling and crisis counseling, there is no place to go for comfort, relief, and peace but to the One who made us and knows us best. We may change the words and try to disguise the true nature of the words we use, but all peace, healing, and nurturing comes from God.

We can re-package His recipe for an abundant, fulfilled life, and we can take credit for having devised our own way to bring about hope and healing. But our ways are woefully inadequate, and the only way true healing will come about is to turn back to God in our schools, our homes, and our workplaces.

As with so much of what God has done for us humans, his answers to youth violence and hatred seem too simple to many of us. We feel that we must revise the tried and true, but our way only ends in frustration and failure.

What is the key to ending violence and bullying? Jesus said it all in John 13:34, "I give you a new commandment, that you love one another."

CLONING: SCIENCE
OR PLAYING GOD?

The fast-paced science of genetics, for all of its positive virtues, brings with it some alarming possibilities. Numerous researchers are experimenting with human cloning, in spite of laws and moral reservations against such research. In fact, the entire explosion of genetic research may usher in a New Millennium version of Huxley's *Brave New World*, in which amazing miracles, heinous evil acts, and mistakes coexist to amaze and frighten us at the same time.

Cracking the genetic code of DNA, a fingerprint in the mystery of life, allows to us identify criminals, deceased persons, and determine paternity. It has also facilitated cloning, producing a genetically identical duplicate of a living entity. Sheep have been cloned, are humans next?

Many people erroneously believe that cloning produces a duplicate with all of the same knowledge, history, abilities, and information. Actually, cloning produces duplicate genes, but the clone is a baby version of the subject, which must grow up and become a person in his or her own right. Animals have inborn instincts, meaning that every offspring or clone has the same instincts and responses to its environment. Humans have a soul and intelligence and discernment. We can communicate and learn to and cope and interact with (and manage) our environment.

The first mammal clone was Dolly, a sheep produced from the genetic material of a six-year-old ewe. Dolly was quickly declared a scientific miracle. She grew up to look and act exactly like her "mother." She also looks and acts like all other sheep. Humans do not look alike, nor do they respond the same way to external stimuli. Recent molecular studies have raised serious questions as to whether Dolly is really a success or a mistake. However, many scientists continue in their concerted effort to clone humans.

A *Washington Post* article stated that Dolly may have been "born old" (*Lansing State Journal* May 27, 1999). Biologists researching Dolly's genetic material found that her telomeres—genetic material at the ends of chromosomes, which become shorter every time a cell divides—have the characteristics of a very old sheep. Many in the scientific community are begging researchers to hold off further human cloning efforts until this and other possible problems can be studied further, but many apparently are ignoring that caution and moving ahead.

A wealthy British lawyer, Mark Hunt, has spent more than 300 British pounds in an effort to clone his son, Andrew, who died at ten months of age following surgery to repair a hole in his heart. After the government closed down a cloning laboratory that was illegally working with the child's tissue, Mr. Hunt immediately began his search for another scientific team willing to bring back his son. At last report, he had retained a lab in West Virginia, run by a group of scientists involved in the Raelian cult, which believes that cloning is the route to mankind's salvation.

Even though the Hunts had another baby recently, he still says that he will, " ... Spend every dime I have to get my son back." He also wrote to a U.S. Congressional Committee investigating human cloning that, "Not since Christ spoke to Lazarus has a human being been able to bridge the great gulf between life and death. I hope my son will be the first." How sad that someone who apparently believes that Christ has power over death still believes that he can play God.

Mankind has attempted many times to become like God. Adam and Eve believed Satan's lie that they would "become like God" if they disobeyed and ate from the forbidden tree. The builders of the Tower of Babel believed they could "build a tower that reaches to heaven ... and make a name for ourselves." Those attempts failed, and so will modern attempts to create life.

When one couples the cloning effort with the fact that mankind daily destroys those God has already created in the womb, our efforts to create life seem even more misdirected. We should focus on using genetics to find more cures and medical advances and leave creation to The Expert.

COMPARISON IS ODIOUS

People often make comparisons between the United States and other countries. We are told that we should pattern our health system after Canada's wonderful government-run system. Closer examination, however, shows that those Canadians who can afford it are flocking across our borders for medical care because of long waiting lists in Canada.

We are often told of Cuba's excellent school system and state-run health program that provides for all medical needs. The truth is that most children are taken from their families at eleven years old and sent to farming communes to work and to be indoctrinated in Communism. That's not exactly the kind of school system Americans should envy. And the quality and access of medical care is not much better than in other third world countries.

Some say we should follow the example of some European countries and legalize hard drugs. Close examination of nearly all of these "successful" drug leniency programs reveals that most of those countries have reversed their stance on legalization. Most of the "free drug use zones," where addicts could use drugs without fear of arrest, have been closed because of rampant crime, including murder and robbery, among the strung-out users.

The United States is often chastised by European nations because some states still sentence criminals to death. The European "Group Against the Death Penalty in the United States" vowed to send a petition containing over one million signatures to Washington, D.C., demanding an end to the death penalty. I don't believe that petition ever arrived.

One European leader stated that it is the world's responsibility to force America into compliance on "such a grave moral issue" as the death penalty. These are the same leaders who promote controversial "morning after" abortion pill, and support abortion on demand. Sometimes, morality is "situational."

The major problem with morality defined from the human perspective is that it is in contrast with what God says. God commands that certain crimes against His and mankind's laws deserve death, but that innocent life should be spared and protected. The world turns this concept on its head, demanding leniency for the guilty and death to the innocent. God requires consequences for bad decisions and behavior outside the bounds of His established law. Mankind believes we should not hold people accountable for their actions, and, in fact, should celebrate decadence.

America remains a mystery to the rest of the world. Most other nations cannot conceive of fifty sovereign states making their own decisions in such matters. No monarchy or parliament decides what takes place in our daily lives. No petition from foreign entities has any effect on the sovereignty of the states.

America was founded by people who desired self-determination and the right to worship and live as they felt was best for them, and the inescapable fact is that our founders did express and declare that their efforts were based upon Judeo Christian tenets.

With all of our shortcomings, most Americans still espouse Christianity, and as long as people keep the lines of communication open with God, there is a hope for His Spirit to right societal wrongs. The Bible declares, in Psalm 33: 12, "Blessed is the nation whose God is the LORD..." We have been blessed, and for our first two hundred years, we strove to adhere to God's commands.

Instead of heeding the counsel of other nations that castigate us for our beliefs, consider that the American Embassy is usually the easiest place to identify in other countries, because of the long lines of people trying to come to America to live. And most of those who signed the petition against the death penalty in the United States would rather live in the U.S. than in their own "enlightened" nation. As a late mentor often said, "Comparison is odious."

THE END OF THE WORLD

It seems only yesterday that we were all stressed out about Y2K. Before we knew it, we had all transitioned, nearly uneventfully, and everything was back to business as usual. The world didn't end, as many feared it would, so the end-days seers had to reset their doomsday clocks. During the uncertain times leading up to January 1, 2000, many people did begin to seriously ponder their mortality. Opinion polls sprang up inquiring as to what people would do if, in fact, the end of the world became date-certain.

The answers to such polls, if taken today, would be decidedly more laid back and worldly than they were in December 1999. But, even in the face of impending kismet, the responses ran the gamut of human emotion, from the silly to the mundane to the reflective.

Many said that they would spend their last hours with their loved ones. Others said they would want to be praying in church when the end came. A majority of respondents stated that they would spend their final hours partying. One guy admitted that he would save a little time for prayer in order to, " ... hedge my bets" (and thereby squeak by, if, by chance prayer does open the pearly gates).

Still others said they would do something that they had always been afraid to do, like cliff-diving, parasailing over the ocean, or skydiving. To some, that which is out of the question when one's life expectancy is unknown becomes a reasonable risk when death is imminent and certain. An alarming number of people said they would spend money like there was no tomorrow, if there was no tomorrow. Apparently, the old phrase "you can't take it with you" still evades many of us.

Some said they would start smoking cigarettes, drink themselves silly, or use illegal drugs. One person said he would pour a glass of champagne, light a candle, and wait for the end. A New York couple said that they would buy a bag of donuts, go up by the river, and eat them and wait. They then said, "Actually, that's what we do on most days, anyway."

Many people would "let it all hang out," with gluttonous eating, illicit sexual acts, or partaking of other forbidden delights the world has to offer. Overall, though, many of the respondents spoke of saving some time for prayer at the end of time.

Some of the responses were comical, some rather pathetic, but these polls spoke volumes about the pitiful view of life and death many people hold. The hard truth is that every second of every hour of every day, someone's world (as he knows it) comes to an end. So it is a perfectly appropriate subject to dwell upon; not so much about our death as about what comes next.

How many people ever really think about life and death? How many ever consider what happens the moment after they take their last breath? Can one know for certain that they will go to Heaven? Since every human being has an eternal soul, and every soul will spend eternity in one of two places, according to the Bible, it would seem that we would want some guarantee.

That guarantee is spelled out in John 3:16, "For God so loved the world, that He gave His only begotten Son, that, whosoever believes in Him shall not perish, but have eternal life."

The doomsday poll illustrates that many people don't know that they can have assurance of eternal life. Christ's final command to believers was to spread His Gospel to all the world, teaching obedience to all that he taught us. That obedience is not demonstrated in seeking last minute worldly delights or final bites of forbidden fruits of sin, but in living a chaste, humble, and penitent life.

We should live every day as though it were our last by focusing on things of Heaven—not the things of this world. The Bible says that believers should not live as citizens of earth, but citizens of Heaven. Many of the responses to these doomsday polls clearly reflect that we have much work to do.

FOUND:
OUR LOST MORAL COMPASS!

Extra! Extra! Read all about it! The lost human moral compass has been located!

A recent scientific study revealed that our moral compass is located behind our foreheads! Like many others, I have often expressed dismay over our nation's lost moral compass. Proving that the moral compass is organic would be a magnificent breakthrough.

According to the study, a key part of the brain's circuitry in back of the forehead helps us learn and obey social rules and morals. Apparently, we would all be nearly perfect, socially responsible, and good, but for head injuries that damage our moral compass and cause us to act out. I quickly scanned the article to make sure a football helmet maker didn't sponsor it.

The study implies that we are all born with intact moral compasses, which are somehow damaged by a head injury at some point before sixteen months, or later in life. The article offered no scientific evidence of its position, so, instead of trying to refute it scientifically, I'd rather look at a few time-tested moral absolutes.

As proof of the location of the human moral compass, the study cited two people, Phineas Gage and an unnamed woman, who were exemplary citizens, until skull injuries turned them into violent malcontents. Gage was injured in 1848 when an explosion caused a metal rod to lodge itself in his prefrontal cortex (forehead). The previously industrious, honest Gage became a profane, lazy drifter.

The author describes the woman as one who was reared in a stable home and had normal intelligence until a forehead injury caused her to engage in petty thievery, habitual lying, and immorality, with no apparent guilt or remorse.

These two examples were the total body of evidence offered by the author, Steven Anderson, who adds, "…the prefrontal cortex is important in using emotions and making decisions. The brain damage keeps people from absorbing lessons taught through reward and punishment in childhood."

While it is true that a closed head injury can alter a person's ability to think and reason, and can even put them into a catatonic or vegetative state, it is quite a stretch to surmise that all bad decisions, bad people, and destructive behavior arise out of a physical injury to a specific part of the body. It appears that the intent of this article is to promote the widely held, politically correct belief that mankind is inherently good, and no one chooses to do wrong. Evil is always the fault of someone or something else.

In contrast, the Bible calls us inherently sinful. Like the article, the Bible cites a human organ, the heart, as the principle initiator of evil and sin. "For out of the heart proceed evil thoughts, murders, adulteries, fornications, thefts, false witness, blasphemies. These are the things that defile man ..." (Matthew 15:19).

The heart mentioned in the scriptures is not the organ in our left chest. It is our "heart of hearts," our conscience, our eternal soul, which is at the center of our being. When the first successful human heart transplants were conducted, many believed the recipient would take on the personality, beliefs and countenance of the donor. Of course, the recipient remained the same person he was prior to the transplant.

Likewise, our moral compass is not located in any organ. A head injury may alter personality or behavior, but a head injury doesn't change a person's morals, or destroy their moral compass.

It is easy to find other organic, hereditary, or societal reasons on which to blame what God defines as simple hostility and rebellion against His rules and commands. If every sin is caused by outside stimuli, then we can't be held accountable. But God created us to be accountable to Him, realizing that we cannot make it without Him. He desires us to flee to Him in repentance, receive His forgiveness and live our lives in His service. Guard your heart, not your forehead!

JAMES J. JACKSON

HARRY POTTER: GOOD VS. EVIL, OR EVIL GLORIFIED?

The great Harry Potter phenomenon is upon us. J.K. Rowling's series of books, upon which the movie of *Harry Potter and the Sorcerer's Stone* is based, has been credited for a new revolution in reading among young children. The books and movie are about an orphan who is found to be a wizard, and subsequently is invited to attend a school of witchcraft and wizardry. The stories are said to captivate the reader.

The movie is filled with the occult, with mystical powers, and with evil, whimsical, and sometimes valiant characters. Many parents apparently believe that any material that captures the attention of children and urges them to read must be of great value. Other parents fear that the content of the books and movie is dangerous on several fronts.

This movie became the second highest grossing film of all time. Many schools bused students to view the movie. Angry parents who did not want their kids to see the movie confronted one such school. Protesters gathered to picket in front of some theaters.

Prominent philosophers and pundits are taking sides on

the Harry Potter issue. Many in the media ridiculed those who expressed concern about the content and the story line, quickly labeling such people as religious fanatics. Christians who state that to allow their children to follow the crowd on this issue would require them to compromise their principles are blasted as being overly protective.

Harry Potter defenders believe the books and movie are harmless, interesting, and thought-provoking, and, therefore, stimulating to the young mind. But, aren't many of these the same people who believe that posting the Ten Commandments in schools is dangerous to young minds? Suppose a school district loaded up the students, without parental permission, and drove them to a Christmas pageant that included the full story of Christ's birth, or to a Passion play detailing Christ's suffering, death and resurrection? Would protesting parents be labeled as fanatics?

The school would be considered in violation of the so-called Constitutional separation of church and state. The same people, however, quickly wink at institutions such as the church of Wicca and the many organized churches for black magic, sorcery, warlocks, etc., which are represented in movies and books such as Harry Potter. Above all, schools should strive to be consistent.

One supporter of the movie stated that he believed Christian virtue is included in the movie, because the underlying theme is "good over evil." But what determines good and evil? Are they concepts that are subject to the fickle human mind? Such human reasoning has brought us "situational ethics," whereby right and wrong are flowing, changeable concepts that are determined by the situation, the whim of the subject, etc. Right and wrong have been established by God, and are not interchangeable.

Christians must be ever vigilant to avoid sending mixed signals to their children. When I was a child, I was taught to always ask where the power comes from in situations concerning magic, the occult, etc. My parents believed that all powers emanate from one of two sources, God or Satan, and that power that glorifies evil, marginalizes, or distorts good, or doesn't glorify God is from Satan.

It is not a secret that confusing good and evil is one of the devil's most common ploys. The Bible warns us, "Woe to those who call good evil and evil good." Everything that sounds benign and harmless is not necessarily so. It is the parent's prerogative to decide what books and movies their children should read or view.

THE SEASONS OF LIFE

In pondering the seasons of life, a dear friend comes to mind. Irene Bergendahl, who died in 2000 at age 102, lived in New York City. She certainly enjoyed the seasons of her life, especially her winter season.

Widowed and childless, Irene's quick wit and razor-sharp mind delighted everyone around her. She had outlived most of her caregivers, friends, and family. She recalled events long past like a human history book. Neither infirmity nor advanced age could convince her to move from the home her late husband, Bill, bought after WWII. She required twenty-four-hour care, but still made most of her daily decisions. Her only regular medication was aspirin to calm "Old Arthur," as she called her arthritis.

When we bought Irene hearing aids, one neighbor opined that it was a waste of money for someone who is "…obviously in the latter stages of her 'winter' season." Irene had few visitors, and spent most days alone, looking out her front window. But we believe that this wonderful friend, who was such an inspiration to our family and countless others, deserved whatever comfort and happiness we could provide for her.

Irene quietly endured the final season of life, but, actually, none of us has a clue as to when we have entered our winter season. Many people mistakenly believe that youth, affluence, or physical wellness assures longevity. But Irene had already outlived many who pitied her as "just an old woman."

In our life cycles, our spring is filled with child's play and discovering our world. (Sadly, many children are never allowed to enter their springtime.) During life's summer, we escape puberty, moving on toward adulthood; gaining wisdom and insight, and making the life decisions that our parents always made for us.

The most pronounced seasonal change, both in nature and in life is from summer to fall (from young adult to middle age). In nature, summer surrenders quickly to the cold, wet, and dreary autumn, with only an occasional respite via a short Indian summer. But the joy of harvest time and the fall colors do serve to warm our spirits. In life, the forty-somethings introduce aches and pains in places where we never knew we had places. Routine chores become challenges. Conversation mostly consists of illness and treatment reports. These bitter physical changes are, theoretically, offset by the maturity and wisdom we (should) acquire with age. Right. Aging is viewed with such disdain today, that many spend their winter season "waiting to die" rather than, as in nature, looking toward renewal.

God ordained seasons in life and in nature, and the pattern will continue as long as He wills it. The Bible says (Ecc. 3) that there is a time to be born; to die; to plant; to reap; to kill; to heal, and so on. Everything has its season. We don't know when our personal winter will come and go. Tomorrow is not promised, so we should live each day as if it were our last.

In nature, winter gives way to the renewal of spring. God intended for mankind to live in a perpetual springtime; a non-stop freshness and newness. But our disobedience brought sin and its death legacy into the world. But, through the sacrifice and resurrection of Jesus Christ, death was defeated. He offers eternal life, which will be forever fresh like Spring, with no pain or suffering, or death, freely to all who trust in Him. All He asks of us in appreciation is to repent of our sins, love one another, and teach others to obey all that He has taught us.

Sound too simplistic? Well, Irene not only believed it with all her heart and soul, but she trusted in Christ alone for her salvation, and she encouraged everyone she knew to live in obedience to Him. She has now gone home to be with the Lord; she will never experience the pains, challenges, or uncertainties of life's winter season again. We should live like we are in our winter, while, like Irene, trusting our eternity to the one called Day Spring.

GUARDING AGAINST LIFE'S OPPORTUNISTS

The onset of several chronic medical conditions over the past few years have been very humbling to me. As a result, I have become very serious about my health, and have learned more about medicine and health management than I ever desired to know.

Some of my medical conditions have reduced my auto-immune system, resulting in frequent skin conditions. The doctor explained that the fine rash that periodically appears on my upper arms is caused by an "opportunistic" virus that would never surface in a person with an intact immune system. The removal of my spleen, which is the largest gland in a person's lymph system, left me vulnerable to recurring, though non-contagious and easily defeated skin irritations.

The doctor went on to explain that many of the plagues and viruses known to mankind still exist, although they have largely been brought under control through vaccination, antibiotics, and other treatments. We are constantly bombarded with various diseases and conditions, most of which are simply conquered by our body's defense mechanisms.

I spent a little time thinking about the many opportunistic entities we often face in daily life, from innocuous skin irritations to life-threatening viruses, bacteria, etc. and from quiet aggression to deadly terrorist attacks. I was reminded of the time when I was a small child and our home had to be quarantined because a cousin who had lived with us had been diagnosed with polio. Polio is highly contagious and easily spread to others. It has been largely removed from all but the most primitive, underdeveloped nations.

Sin and evil operate in opportunistic fashion. A sin area may enter a person's life almost undetected, such as having a penchant for little white lies or gluttony or materialism or fear, or a multitude of other oblique wrong attitudes and actions that we often allow to become a regular part of our life.

Subtle sin can be opportunistic in that it is often easily overlooked, ignored, or minimized, but it can still result in devastation in a person's spiritual life, and in relationships as well. Subtle sin that is indulged and not rooted out through repentance and a concerted effort to turn away from it can prohibit one from experiencing all that the Lord may have in store for him.

Evil, because it often includes the component of intent, may be less subtle, but is even more opportunistic, in that a person must be more proactive at every stage, such as with the terrorists who carefully conceived, planned, and carried out the murders of thousands of civilian Americans.

Evil, much like deadly disease, looks for an entry point, then moves deliberately toward its target, wreaking havoc without mercy, until it is rooted out and rendered powerless. As with terrorists, or even domestic crime, we must be vigilant, and take steps to avoid becoming a victim of evil.

Many teachers of the Bible warn us against allowing sin areas in our lives to "steal our joy." It is depressing and defeating to continually live in one or more sin areas because it separates us from God's best and makes it difficult to receive the grace He has in store for us.

The Bible warns us about Satan's opportunistic approach in 1 Peter 5:8, "Be sober, be vigilant; because the devil, as a roaring lion, walketh about, seeking whom he may destroy." We must be on guard for opportunistic medical conditions and germs, but we must even more so be wary of opportunistic sin and evil, both from within us and externally.

We must put on the whole armor of God in order to always be prepared for the onslaught of sin and evil, which are always looking for an entry way into our lives and hearts.

ACCEPTING RESPONSIBILITY; WHAT A NOVEL CONCEPT!

Taking responsibility. When did such a concept become so rare as it is today? On a recent radio talk show, a caller stated that her seven-year-old son had climbed upon a display, which toppled and injured him slightly. The store's attorney called and offered a large settlement (to avoid future litigation). The mother refused the money, since her son was responsible, calling his injury a consequence for his actions.

The company sent the money anyway. The mom asked whether to send the money back. The talk show host suggested donating the money to charity, and was so impressed with the family's integrity that she offered the family several gifts as an encouragement for taking such an admirable (and rare) stance.

Later, a group of workers were later discussing the situation. Their opinions ranged from incredulity at the "stupidity" of the woman for being honest, to admiration of such a family that would be willing to forego money in order to teach a valuable life lesson to their children.

How sad, that in today's "enlightened" era, a person who

takes the high moral road, instead of sinking to greed and selfishness, is considered stupid, while dishonest people who mock decency are held out as heroes.

Another woman purchased a cup of coffee at a restaurant drive-thru window, then balanced the coffee between her knees. As she drove away, the coffee spilled over and burned her. She sued the restaurant, and was awarded several million dollars by a jury. Many people consider her actions heroic.

In another bewildering instance of out of control litigation, a criminal became stuck in a chimney while attempting to burglarize a business, sued, and was awarded a large sum because the business did not maintain the chimney in a safe manner. Nothing was said about the fact he was breaking in, or that the chimney was never intended as an entrance to the business.

When I was a child, my parents taught us that taking responsibility for our actions would result in some measure of leniency, while refusing to take responsibility could cause stricter sanctions. They did not remove consequences when we admitted guilt, but punishment was much greater if the truth had to be extracted from us. The penalty was most severe for standing in denial while allowing someone else to be punished for your infraction. Taking responsibility is distasteful. It rages against our human nature. The Bible says we inherited our nature from Adam, the first man God created.

When God asked why he had eaten from the forbidden tree, Adam said, "The woman you put here with me—she gave me some fruit from the tree, and I ate it" (Gen. 3:12). Perhaps we would all still be living in the Garden of Eden, had Adam simply stated, "I have violated your rules. Please forgive me."

Taking responsibility means agreeing that we have done wrong. The biblical concept of repentance, upon which our judicial process is, in large part, based, means acknowledging that we have violated a rule or law. As with my parents, a court is likely to be more lenient when an offender admits responsibility. In many cases, the person may avoid the death penalty by telling the truth in court.

An even greater step than admitting responsibility for one's own shortcomings is taking the blame and punishment for someone else's actions, when you are blameless. This goes against every fiber of our human existence, yet someone did just that, for all of us.

Because we all inherited Adam's sinful nature, and none of us can be good enough to save ourselves, Christ came into the world, lived a perfect life, paid the price for all sin, and now offers eternal life to all who believe in Him. Taking responsibility and repenting for our wrongs and receiving God's forgiveness helps us to understand the unwarranted but unconditional love God has for His creation.

THE FUTILITY OF 'TIME MANAGEMENT'

Anyone who's been double-scheduled for meetings knows that time management is pretty much an oxymoron. Today, we all strive to gain control of our time. Gadget gurus provide time management tools, such as the Palm Pilot, to help us track everything from appointments and meetings to stock quotes and email. But even state-of-the-art electronics can't give us control of time.

When I retired from a fast-paced executive position, I vowed to finally control my time. Not! In very short order, I have incrementally filled 150% of the available time with new "required activities." So, my time is still not my own.

A friend suggested I get a cellular phone and a day-timer with an alarm to remind me of an imminent obligation. Then, I would be in control of my time. But, if my telephone, fax machine, and email haven't put me in control of my time, how can another apparatus be anything more than another electronic tether? I am retired, for goodness sake!

So, even in retirement, the time problem isn't resolved. I always planned to do basically anything I wanted to do. I was going to fish more, read more, finish writing the great American novel, get it published and marketed, and so on. I do spend more time with the grandkids, but I haven't fished much, and, other than obligatory reading responsibilities, and an occasional hour or two of novel reading each week, I don't seem to find time to devour books as I had planned. I haven't even looked at my novel since retirement.

The whole concept of time changes constantly throughout our life span. Children can't wait to grow up to partake of "grown up" activities and privileges. But, many adults, once given a taste of being grown up, want to recapture their youth. Young adults long to find true love and get married, but the divorce and separation statistics point out that few find the bliss they may have anticipated and hoped for.

Married couples long for children, and many regret it once they realize that rearing children is not a cakewalk. We can't wait for our children to grow up, and then we bemoan how fast time flew. And then there's the grandchildren. We want them to stay sweet and cuddly. We don't want to watch them face the challenges and pains of growing up and facing an ever-changing world.

We sense an urgency to teach them and warn them against bad behavior, bad habits, and bad people. Reality sets in abruptly when we realize that we are at the age our grandparents were when we considered them "old." The time between the "invincible" days of youth and middle age passes so fast, it makes one's head spin (or is it the blood pressure again?).

As a teenager, I would read the obituary of a fifty or sixty-year-old person, and I would think to myself, *Did he think he would live forever?* Now, at fifty-one, I read about a seventy-five-year-old, and think, *He wasn't very old!* A dear friend, Irene Bergendahl, died recently, at age 102. She was alert and active until the end, with no chronic illnesses. While thinking about the abnormally long life she had been blessed with, I realized that I am half her age! Depressing? Not at all.

At Irene's funeral, we reflected upon her faith and how she trusted in the words in "Amazing Grace," which says that when we've been in Heaven 10,000 years, we will have "…no less days to sing God's praise than when we'd first begun…" It really takes the edge off when we view life in eternal terms. The urgency remains, although for different reasons. I feel an urgency to tell others what Christ said in 1 John 11:26, "And whosoever liveth and believeth in me shall never die. Believest thou this?" I believe, and I want to tell others while there is still Time.

THE KEY TO GOOD
RACE RELATIONS

Emmett Till was a distant cousin of mine. His lynching had a profound influence in shaping my life.

You might think it would have made our family bitter. That's what people automatically think should happen. But our reaction was much more complex than that.

Emmett's widowed mother, Mamie, and my father, Sam Jackson, were first cousins who grew up in Mississippi before seeking a better life in Chicago. During that time, many parents sent their children from the cities to spend the summers with relatives in the South. Groups of fathers and uncles would travel south in caravans, returning in late August to pick up the children.

When Emmett was killed in 1955, seven of my siblings were in a nearby town, Hazelhurst, visiting our grandparents. My younger brother, one sister, and I stayed home. My uncle, along with several other men, drove from Chicago to Mississippi, dropping children off in places like Money, where Emmett's grandparents lived, and Hazelhurst, where my grandparents lived as share-croppers. Blacks could not rent motel or hotel rooms along the way and could only stop at service stations with "Colored facilities."

The travelers packed items that would keep, such as bread, crackers and cheese, fried chicken and cakes, and jugs of water (not every town had "Colored" water fountains). Some of the states along the way provided "'road-side stands'" for such travelers. These pull-offs consisted of one or two picnic tables and a trash can; a place to pull off and stretch and, perhaps, change drivers.

In the minds of the children, this was just an exciting adventure, but the adults had to be ever-vigilant for racist KKK members, or car loads of teens looking for trouble. They rarely tarried long at any place, driving almost non-stop to their destination. After Emmett was murdered, there was a mad scramble of concerned fathers and others who drove south to bring the children back home. The confusion and anger was frightening for me as a six-year-old. I also remember the sad open-casket funeral.

February is Black History Month, and Emmett Till is a part of my history and of all our history. But too many people use this month to dwell upon the discrimination that still exists and spend too much time looking for bigotry in every situation. Many black leaders encourage people to ignore signs of true progress in race relations.

We should reflect on the struggles our forebears endured. But it draws us down when we continue to live in that era; ignoring changes and living in a "slave mentality," which hinders us from moving forward. In my own life, I've faced many instances of prejudice and racism, but my parents always put it in the right perspective. I was taught to pray for those who offended me, and to figure out a way around a situation or to ask for grace to endure it. My Aunt Bessie, who raised us after our parents' deaths, taught us a saying—"This, too, shall pass," which has brought me spiritual peace many times during my life.

I was taught that prejudice will always exist, as long as sinful mankind exists, but that I must never allow it to define me, confine me, or stop me from seeking success. That has been the theme by which I have lived my life, and success has come through seeking excellence and not allowing others to limit or determine my success.

Most importantly, I was also taught that Jesus gave a new Commandment that encompasses all of the original ten: "Love one Another." Failure to follow that command is the root of all prejudice. If we all apply that one key, it will go a long way toward ending all prejudice.

DEATH LOSES ITS STING
FOR ALS VICTIM

Death is something of a morbid topic, and many would rather not even think of death, while others spend much of their time worrying about death and wondering when the Grim Reaper may visit them.

When I was in my teens, I often read the obituary page in the newspaper. I would spot someone who died at age fifty or sixty, and I would think, "Wow, were they old! Did he or she think they would live forever?" Now, in my fifties, when I read about the death of someone in their seventies, or even eighties, I think, "They were so young!"

Age is very relative. The obituaries include people from infancy to those over one hundred years of age. The reader's heart aches for the parents who have lost a newborn or very young child, although it is impossible to really empathize unless one has actually experienced it.

Many obit writers take pains to say that the deceased was not just a statistic, but a vital, much-loved part of a family. They list the deceased's accomplishments and survivors. Many express the deceased's faith in Christ; others simply announce the death, with no indication as to what the person believed or much else about him or her.

The Bible teaches us to take measure of our lives and to give thanks in all circumstances. A few years ago, a friend, Kevin, was diagnosed with ALS, known as Lou Gehrig's Disease. His physician advised him what to expect; the disease is fatal, and Kevin would slowly lose strength in his arms and legs and spine. He would soon lose his ability to walk or move at all. His brain, however, would remain intact and strong, witnessing the wasting of his body. Most victims live from one to four years from diagnosis, and usually die when the throat muscles collapse and suffocation occurs.

Kevin, in his late thirties, took a disability retirement from his job and went home dreading what had befallen him. At first, he was angry, wondering why God hated him so. Then he felt despair. As he turned down his street, Kevin drove past a neighbor, Matt, out for a run. Matt, a strong, vibrant young man, smiled and waved at Kevin as he passed by. Kevin waved back, and, in depths of despondency, shouted out loud, "I would almost give my soul if I could change places with Matt right now!"

Kevin lived about four years, during which he learned to paint and write with some of the technological tools invented for ALS patients. He watched his children grow into teens, and was able to share many life lessons with them. He was nourished and cared for by his loving, supportive wife, Kerri. He had never had much of a worship life, until one day at therapy he met another ALS patient who seemed all too happy for someone facing such a disastrous future.

This man, Mel, told Kevin that he believed that all things work for good in those who love the Lord and shared the Gospel message with Kevin. Mel stated that after he was diagnosed with ALS he began reading the Book of Job, and he had adopted a passage from it as his source of strength, "Though he slay me, yet will I hope in him; I will surely defend my ways to his face."

Kevin prayed to receive the free gift of eternal life that Jesus had paid for with His death, and he began to see his life through different eyes. He found out that his neighbor, Matt, had been struck by a car and killed shortly after passing by on the same day when Kevin had dreamed of changing places with him.

Kevin knew then that God had allowed him to have ALS so that he could come to know Christ as his savior, and had God granted his wish Kevin would have had only a few moments to live, and would have missed out on so much. He adopted a verse from Matthew as his source of strength for the remainder of his life, Matt 6:27: "Who of you by worrying can add a single hour to his life?"

NO DOUBT ABOUT IT:
CHRIST AROSE!

D on't be fertile ground for seeds of doubt.

One of Satan's most powerful tools is doubt. He uses it to create confusion and fear in our lives. He tried to use doubt to tempt Jesus in the wilderness. He hoped that the human body God had taken on was so weakened by hunger and thirst, that perhaps a small seed of doubt would quickly grow and destroy God's plan of salvation for us humans. Christ repelled Satan with the truth of the Holy Scriptures.

Doubt is like the twin of a lie, which makes it even more important to know the truth. When I worked for the Federal Reserve Bank, counterfeit enforcement agents learned to detect counterfeit bills, not by learning every fraud method, but by studying and learning legitimate currency so well, that a bad one would stick out like a sore thumb. This is the Christian approach to biblical frauds that pop up so often.

Satan's seeds of doubt are intended to stop us from trusting in the Lord. Doubt tries to make us waiver in our faith by instilling worry and despair, whispering suggestively that

God no longer loves us, so we may as well seek our own way.

Satan uses all manner of deception to plant seeds of doubt in the lives of God's people. He doesn't need to plant doubt in unbelieving agnostics and atheists. Many, by their rejection of God's love, already belong to Satan, and are useful to him in spreading the seeds.

A recently released film promotes the lie that Christ did not die or rise from the dead, but married and had a child before dying like any other man. It claims to have found the family's burial site, which is vehemently disputed by Christian scholars and Jewish historians, alike.

The entertainment media have alarming influence over people's lives and have taken the lead in attempting to disparage the truth of the Bible, thereby destroying established, irrefutable historical data simply by raising doubt. Films such as *The Last Temptation of Christ*, and *The DaVinci Code*, and this latest documentary depicting Jesus as a sinful mortal are simply blasphemous attempts to destroy the truth that Christ as Savior and Lord.

The Bible says (and secular historians have validated) that Jesus was crucified, died, was buried, and was resurrected. Throughout the years, some have raised the prospect that Jesus was not crucified, but traveled across Asia, and died in Kashmir, India. The first people to doubt Jesus' resurrection were the Jewish leaders themselves, who claimed the disciples stole the body and hid it.

They searched extensively for proof, but found none. The testimony of the Romans soldiers, who were struck with fear and frozen in place as the heavy stone was mysteriously rolled away, played a large part in establishing the truth of the resurrection.

Had either the Romans or the Jewish leaders been able to find a sliver of doubt as to the resurrection, they would have exploited it to the hilt. Jesus' disciples endured torture and death while steadfastly insisting upon the truth of the resurrection. Someone certainly would have admitted it was a hoax, if that were so.

Also, the writings of contemporary Roman historians from that era have long been considered concise and complete; however, not one of them questioned the veracity of the story of Jesus' crucifixion, death, burial and resurrection. No one in history has been so thoroughly investigated, doubted, and demeaned, but no one else has revealed himself to be so powerful in the lives of so many.

Jesus, Himself, said it best, "... I am the resurrection and the life. He who believes in me will live, even though he dies..." The Triune God even creates the faith to believe in Him. He also tells us that those who try to lead His sheep away from Him will one day face the punishment for their sins.

Many religions threaten death to anyone who blasphemes their gods. Why aren't Christians rising up and protesting this latest fraud? God doesn't need our defense. He is Almighty. Learn God's truth, as written in the Bible, and the frauds will have no effect on you, because those seeds of doubt will find no fertile ground in your heart.

MOTHERS ENDURE
ALL THINGS

May is the month in which we set aside a day to honor mothers. Of all of God's creations, mothers are a cut above. Mothers bring forth into the world all manner of people, or step into the job of rearing someone who is in need of a mother. Most of us have fond memories of our mothers as we grew up, taking us places, feeding, and clothing us.

We remember the unconditional love, the hugs, kisses, the warm smile, the caring touch. We remember how she actually felt the pain when we got hurt. We remember growing from a totally dependent state to the independent teen age state and into adulthood. We remember Mother's beaming pride she showed whenever we experienced even the slightest accomplishment.

Fathers have more of a capacity of being aloof, noncommittal, even indifferent toward their children, but God somehow gave mothers an unbreakable bond to their children. Mothers always try to put the best construction on their children's actions and decisions. Mothers light up at the mere thought of one of their children.

Mothers have been blessed with the capacity to love deeper, suffer more, care more, and endure more pain than a father ever could. Mothers spend time trying to shape their child into a good citizen, but will always be there if the child fails. When describing her child, a mother will struggle to find kind adjectives to mask those traits that might seem less than desirable, while lathering on praise for those actions that are impressive. Many mothers spend most of their lives on their knees, praying for the well-being of their children.

Sometimes we lead lives that honor our mothers, and make them proud of us. Sometimes people bring shame upon their mothers by their actions. Often, the child eventually asks for forgiveness, and reconciles with his mother.

But, imagine the plight of the mothers of those who wreak havoc and destruction upon innocent people. Imagine the unspeakable pain and agony felt by the mothers of Timothy McVeigh, or of Cho Seung-Hui, the Virginia Tech murderer. Imagine the dismay that comes from knowing that someone you reared, loved, and nurtured, somehow developed such hatred, rage, or evil in his or her heart that drove him to seek and destroy any human life that wandered across his path.

While it is difficult for some people to have any compassion for the perpetrator who took the time to calculate, plan, and carry out the deed, it is often easy to ignore or dispatch thoughts of the people in the murderer's life who have to live with the aftermath. Cho's parents tell of having to go into hiding for fear of retribution from others for their son's actions.

Imagine the questions that will never be answered.

Imagine the strange dichotomy of holding the deep mother love in your heart that is being crowded out by the bitter hatred of the deed your loving offspring has done. It would seem that those who plan and carry out heinous acts must first suppress any thoughts of what the act will do to the person's mother. It is hard to believe that one could carry out murderous acts without worrying about the effect upon his or her family, particularly his or her mother.

Even when faced with a small indiscretion, I usually consider the effect it may have upon the memory of my mother, and I will refrain, rather than bring dishonor upon her memory. It's sad that so many people seem to be able to ignore the likely effect upon their family, particularly upon the one who bore them and tried to rear them honorably. Even a mother who might be described as a bad parent usually desires the best for her children.

For McVeigh and Cho to take such actions, they must have first denounced the Biblical admonishment to Honor your Mother and Father. On this Mother's Day, please pray for peace and comfort for all others mothers, especially the mothers of such as these.

FALWELL STOOD IN THE GAP

When the news of Jerry Falwell's death broke, I found it interesting that, of all of the great accomplishments in this man's life, the media chose to point out his misstatements and flaws.

He once mused that a PBS Teletubby named Tinky-Winkie may have been devised to promote the gay agenda. He also founded and led the 25,000-student Liberty University in Lynchburg, Virginia. The Teletubby story was front and center in the report of Falwell's passing. Liberty University wasn't mentioned.

In the 1970s, Falwell noted that immorality was beginning to surface as the norm, while moral living was ridiculed. He believed that most people were good and moral citizens, so he formed the group and coined the phrase, "The Moral Majority," and began a life-long effort to take on the elements in society that he viewed as anti-moral and anti-God.

The Moral Majority grew to become a successful lobbying group for God's perspective on major legislation. In Ezekiel, God says, "I looked for a man among them who would build up the wall and stand before me in the gap on behalf of the land." Jerry Falwell tried to be that someone who would "stand in the gap" between right and wrong, declaring what God has established as right, and refusing to allow the lines to become blurred.

At Liberty University, Falwell proved that young people can receive a quality education without the social programming that is inherent in public education. Students are provided a biblically-based education, and the proof is in the pudding, as the saying goes. Many alumni have gone on to become viable forces within the legal, educational, and medical communities.

Falwell also established the 22,000-member Thomas Road Baptist Church, a theological seminary, and a correspondence school. Falwell was human, and thereby subject to occasional errors in judgment, but it seems that the media insist upon elevating the few controversial sound bites to try to define Falwell as some kind of religious fanatic who shoots from the lip.

Nothing could be further from the truth. Sometimes, in his zeal to defend things spiritual, Falwell might have used language that could be construed as strong, but he was big enough to apologize when that happened. When we were attacked on September 11, 2001, Falwell was vilified in the press for blaming the attacks on pagans, abortionists, feminists, gays, lesbians, the American Civil Liberties Union, and People For The American Way, saying, "I point the finger in their face and say 'you helped this happen.'" He later apologized for naming specific groups, stating that such groups may have contributed to the creation of " ... an environment which possibly has caused God to lift the veil of protection which has allowed no one to attack America on our soil since 1812."

He also opined that such attacks could be God's judgment on America for "throwing God out of the public square, out of the schools. The abortionists have got to bear some burden for this because God will not be mocked." Later, he stated that only the hijackers and terrorists were responsible for the deadly attacks. He also said, "I do believe, as a theologian, based upon many Scriptures and particularly Proverbs 14:34, which says 'Righteousness exalts a nation, but sin is a disgrace to any people.'"

While the major media would rather report derogatory items about Rev. Falwell, there was much more to his life than those missteps. He was a humble man who cared about others. Many former Liberty students tell stories of Falwell personally helping them financially, through counseling, or just with moral support.

Whether one agrees with Rev. Falwell's politics or religious beliefs, his service to others cannot be denied. We are all sinners and subject to saying things that we really don't mean, but the true measure of a person is the fruits of his labor. I believe that Falwell's legacy is one of faith and doing God's work to the best of his ability. All Christians, regardless of denomination, should strive to serve others as Jerry Falwell did, and to seek opportunities to stand in the gap for what's right.

IS THE CHRISTMAS TREE
A PAGAN SYMBOL? WAY!

A group recently launched an effort to end the use of Christmas trees, calling them a pagan expression. The spokesman stated that we are wasting millions of trees for the sake of pagan expression. Could this group have entirely missed the point of Christmas?

We don't worship the Christmas tree, or believe it to be a symbol to be honored or revered. Rather, it is a traditional item used in the overall celebration of Christmas. The simple fact that an evergreen tree was once used in pagan ceremonies, or that non-Christians once placed lights in trees to honor their gods does not mean that our seasonal use of the tree is pagan in origin.

Candles are traditionally used in Christian church worship. They were (and are) used in pagan worship. Does this mean candle-lit Christian worship services are pagan? It is deceptive to imply that the use of an item or tradition that may have been used by pagans renders that use as pagan.

Actually, the approach of reducing Christianity to the level of the worship of false gods is not new. If taken to its logical conclusion, Christians should cease using the names of days and months, since many of them came from Roman and Greek gods. Should Christians refuse to call Thursday by its name, since it name gives attribution to the Norse god Thor, the god of thunder?

Should we reject the month of January, since it was named for the god Janus, who was supposedly able to look both backward and forward? Or May, named to honor the mother of Mercury? Or Wednesday, named for the god Odin (or Woden), god of magic?

I collect swords. Swords have certainly been used in paganism, mysticism, and even satanic worship. I don't use my swords in any such manner, so the usage and my attitude toward the sword are what matters, not the many misuses that may have occurred in the past by others. To think that I should not possess swords because they have been used for ungodly purposes in the past is patently absurd.

Actually, it is impossible to choose a date or item to use as part of any celebration that has not been first used in some kind of pagan worship. Therefore, the emphasis should be on the reason for using a date or an item. The Christmas tree is a part of long-standing tradition, and is not worshiped.

The most vocal opponents of Christmas trees seem to be more worried about the cutting down of trees than on whether it is a proper expression of Christianity. They seem to omit the clear truth that, pageantry and symbolism aside, the true meaning of Christmas stands strong and all-powerful.

Christmas, unlike the many expressions of paganism, expresses the fulfillment of centuries of prophecy, the promise God made to fallen mankind—that we are all sinful and incapable of saving ourselves. In His infinite wisdom and unmerited love for us, His Word, which was and is and always will be a part of Him, became human in the person of Jesus Christ to show us the way to salvation from our sins. Only true man and true God could pay the price for our sin and then offer eternity freely to those who trust in Him. The Bible tells us that the wages of sin is death, but the *gift* of God is eternal life.

This marvelous gift was delivered to us through the birth, sinless life, death, and resurrection of the child who was born humbly on that Christmas night. Paganism has nothing to do with it. Christmas trees show us that light came into a dark world through Christ's birth, and trees and other traditional items add to the celebration of this miracle.

BACK TO SCHOOL IN THE NEW MILLENNIUM

Remember those exciting back-to-school days at summer's end? The smell of new clothes, shoes, pencils and paper, newly painted classrooms. Backpacks depicting sports or cartoon heroes were proudly strapped on. Parents hoped their child would be a good student and get along with others. In the new millennium, however, going back to school has taken on a totally new dynamic.

Today's required school supplies include see-through backpacks (for easy weapons/explosives detection), and clothing without metal buckles that could trigger the metal detector. Maybe a cellular phone to call 911, if necessary. Photo ID cards must be worn. Parents fear they may never see their kids alive again, that their child's school will be the next to experience murder and mayhem. The stress level is extremely high. What should be a happy, enjoyable time for families is, instead, filled with a morbid fear that steals their joy.

School districts used to hire teachers and substitutes, maintenance and other support staff, but in the nineties, schools must also have professional grief counselors on standby in case of a catastrophe or violence. The grief counselors' job is a formidable undertaking in light of the restrictions they operate under. One dilemma is which perspective to express in counseling victims of tragedy. They cannot label any action as "sin," and this distorts the concepts of right and wrong. They instead try blame someone or something else for the perpetrators' actions (…they were picked on, were medicated, acted out of revenge, etc.). Any excuse will do, as long as the perpetrator's actions are not labeled "evil."

Counselors cannot invoke God in the discussion, lest they violate the separation of church and state dictum. But how can an act be declared right or wrong, good or bad without citing the authoritative source for such a declaration? Children, well aware of adults' faults, are rightfully reluctant to look to us for answers or blindly accept our concept of right and wrong. But a counselor is restricted from telling children about a God who, out of love for them, established certain standards of right and wrong.

How do experts address death without invoking anything "religious"? Do they give the kids today's psychobabble response that death is "just another part of life"? They can't even tell kids that God says, "Thou shall not commit murder." How do they calm the fears of kids who have been victimized or are fearful of being victimized by violence? It is painfully obvious to children, as more instances of school violence occur, that their teachers and others are incapable of protecting them.

Counselors are precluded from discussing concepts like the courage of conviction demonstrated by young people who died rather than recant their faith in the Lord. Do they paint these victims as martyrs, or as people who should have told the gunmen what they wanted to hear, in order to save their lives? Secular counselors teach the victims to turn inward for answers. But without God, all they find inside is more grief, more disappointment, and more despair.

Secular humanism cannot comprehend the level of faith demonstrated by the girl who, faced with death, declared her love for the Lord, refusing to deny God to save her own life. Christ says, in Matthew 10, "He who finds his life will lose it, and he who loses his life for my sake will find it." God also tells us to, "Set your mind on things above, not on things on the earth," (Col. 3:2). This includes life, itself. For a believer, life doesn't really begin until we reach Heaven, so a believer doesn't fear what man can do to him. Someone once said, "Fear knocked; faith answered ... no one was there."

Can counselors provide hope? Hope doesn't come from metal detectors or more laws. Every perpetrator violates numerous laws already on the books. God's word teaches us that murder and mayhem begin in the heart. He wants us to guide our children to ask Him to come into their hearts. But counselors are required to view God and His love as more dangerous than a murderer.

Counselors are not allowed to tell children about the one who really brings about healing and hope, so they are left with a failed methodology. There is fierce resistance to the suggestion of posting the Ten Commandments in schools. God is the only answer for our schools. Secular approaches to solving problems only lead to more questions than answers and more hopelessness and fear than before, and as long as we insist on doing it man's way, the results will always be the same.

HOSPICE: ANGELS ON EARTH

We often hear about unsung heroes who use their time and talents to serve others. There are many agencies and organizations that regularly meet the needs of others, but there is one organization that rises above and beyond the normal call to assist others.

Hospice is a nationwide network of independent, non-profit organizations that, according to Hospice literature, "… provides care to those facing the end of their life, regardless of the diagnosis or ability to pay…" I have had several friends who have utilized the services of hospice for a dying loved one, and I know that those services go well beyond their mission statement.

Hospice allows a patient to experience comfort, dignity, and peace during the last stages of life. More than that, Hospice fulfills the needs of the family and extended family of the dying. They provide psychological and spiritual counselors to help families cope with the emotional and physical strain of watching a loved one suffer.

They work with the patient's medical insurance provider to provide medical equipment and supplies. If the patient is uninsured, the needed items are provided free, and usually delivered to the patient's home or hospital room. They depend upon donations in order to provide for services and supplies not covered by insurance. Unlike hospitals, whose services end with the death of the patient, Hospice provides grief counseling to family and friends for at least thirteen months after the patient's death.

Hospice also provides volunteer support to perform household chores, run errands, or sit with the patient to give the family respite. Hospice accepts patients who are in the last stages of illnesses such as Alzheimer's, in which diagnosis of when the patient is truly terminal is difficult. Death may appear imminent, but the patient may rebound and seem physically and medically sound. Hospice provides a kit, which is to be used at certain intervals and in the presence of certain conditions, in order to assure that the patient is as comfortable and pain-free as possible as the dying process continues.

Hospice provides twenty-four-hour access to a hospice nurse (not an answering service), twenty-four hours per day, seven days per week, as well as full-time staff physicians certified in hospice care, including pediatric hospice for terminally ill children. They serve any patient who is terminally ill, whether or not the patient has a primary caregiver, and even if the patient is receiving dialysis, chemotherapy, radiation, or tube-feeding.

Many hospice agencies around the country maintain a "Hospice House," where patients spend their last days in a serene, quiet, comfortable environment, surrounded by family and friends, pets, or whatever they need to keep the patient peaceful and happy. Hospitals, on the other hand, must provide services to other patients, and do not usually allow large numbers of family members to come in until the patient is very near death. Hospice provides a large, beautifully decorated room and pleasant background music and encourages family to be close to the patient.

Hospice provides transportation for patients living at home, and a nurse is assigned to the patient to meet his/her needs. While there are a multitude of social agencies that provide assistance to families and the infirm, hospice goes above and beyond to assist the patient and the family. They are truly angels on earth.

In Matthew 26, when Christ lauded His disciples for feeding Him and giving Him something to drink when He was hungry and thirsty, clothing Him and visiting Him when He was sick, etc., the disciples inquired as to when they had done these things, and Jesus answered, "When you have done these things for one of the least of these my brethren, you have done it for me."

Support Hospice. They fulfill this passage.

TEN COMMANDMENTS CASE
AFFECTS ALL OF OUR RIGHTS

Alabama Supreme Court Chief Justice Roy Moore placed a monument to the Ten Commandments in the lobby of the Supreme Court building in Montgomery. This raised the ire of leftists, atheists, and the American Civil Liberties Union for more than two years.

He refused to remove the monument after a federal judge ruled it violated the constitutional "separation of church and state." A state judicial panel suspended him. Moore filed suit to block the removal of the 5,300-pound monument, but it was removed several hours before a scheduled hearing on the lawsuit.

Those who cheer such judicial activism and the type that prohibits graduates from honoring or acknowledging God in commencement addresses should be wary of the new ground they may be breaking. While celebrating the goring by someone else's ox, one may be inadvertently exposing one's own flank to the same fate.

I often wonder if those on the left have really thought

out their position on the so-called separation of church and state.

First, there is no mention in the U.S. Constitution of a separation of church and state. The founders' intent was to protect religious practice from government, not the other way around. The current practice of picking and choosing which freedoms we will defend could set a dangerous precedent when attacks against freedom of speech other than religious speech arise. How do we stop activists from bastardizing the remaining tenets of the U.S. Constitution by changing words and meanings and adding nonexistent phrases?

The freedom of the press allows the print media to write whatever they desire and to withhold information about sources, etc. Now that we have opened the gate to judicial fiat, such constitutional freedoms are just as vulnerable as the "establishment of religion" clause. Likewise, the free speech clause can be distorted to mean whatever a judge decides it means.

The First Amendment states, "Congress shall make no law respecting an establishment of religion, or prohibiting the free exercise thereof; or abridging the freedom of speech, or of the press; or the right of the people peaceably to assemble, and to petition the Government for a redress of grievances."

It is foolish to believe that, once we allow an activist judge to usurp any portion of the Constitution, those portions that we personally hold dear will be safe from the same activism. If the intent of any portion of the Constitution can be changed to satisfy a particular agenda, then every part of our founding documents is just as vulnerable.

We must demand the integrity of our founding documents. Changing the intent by adding words that do not exist in the document opens the entire document to individual judicial interpretation.

If a judge opined that the "free press" wording only means that media outlets cannot be owned by government, and therefore, editorials must take a government-directed slant, an uproar would ensue. Or if it was determined that freedom of speech only referred to private conversations between two people, and did not include freedom of expression, people would be ready to revolt.

By our silence about attacks against any part of any amendment, we give tacit approval in advance to a future activist court to do to free speech, the press, and the freedom to redress our government what they are currently doing to the religious clause.

Judge Moore stated, "I cannot forsake my conscience." We do so at our peril.

FORGIVENESS AND TIMOTHY MCVEIGH

Timothy McVeigh, to the very end, felt that what he had done was justified. While it is often difficult to ascertain a person's stand on crucial issues at the time of death, McVeigh left little mystery about his lack of remorse or his stoic belief that destroying the Oklahoma City federal building and the lives of so many people was justified.

McVeigh angered many people by calling the children he murdered, "collateral damage," as if their deaths meant no more to him than the building, vehicles or other "incidental" objects destroyed by the blast. His refusal to show any remorse, even to the end, added fuel to that fire.

Some of his injured victims, and some of the survivors of those who died, have publicly forgiven him for what he did, even though he, in sheer defiance, refused to ask for forgiveness. Others have stated that they will never forgive him.

Forgiveness does as much, if not more, for the forgiver as for the forgiven. It releases one from the bondage of holding a grudge. It takes a concerted effort to continue to despise and hate someone, regardless of how evil and cruel that person is.

One who refuses to forgive must daily renew his hatred for the perpetrator, much as McVeigh had to strive every day from the conception to the completion of his crime, to maintain his level of anger and rage with anyone and anything connected with the government.

Forgiving even an unrepentant person releases the forgiver from a net of emotional captivity. Much more, it demonstrates to all the concept of grace. God forgives us when we wrong Him, which we all do with regularity. We deserve eternal punishment for our sins, yet He accepts our repentance unconditionally.

McVeigh called himself an agnostic, stating that if after death he found that there was a God, he would "improvise." How could a person who seems to have had a normal American upbringing sink to such a stage in his spiritual life that human life has so little value when measured against his chosen agenda?

McVeigh only said he was sorry that so many "had to die" for his cause. He even chose a tough-sounding excerpt from the nineteenth century poem, "Invictus," for his final statement, which in part, intones, " ... I am the master of my fate. I am the captain of my soul."

How could McVeigh become so callous in such a short lifespan as to have embraced such twisted logic in order to massacre so many innocent children and adults because he believed the government he loathed murdered children in Waco?

There are so many more questions than answers in the McVeigh saga, many of which may never be answered. Apparently he did not know that there is a God who prohibits us from taking revenge, since He is the only one just and merciful enough to do so. He either ignored or did not know that there is a God who says we should not murder, regardless of our emotions or anger toward others.

McVeigh apparently didn't understand that while our decisions here on earth may affect circumstances and consequences while we live, none of us is the master of his eternal fate or the captain of his eternal soul. Our final fate rests with God.

In Matthew, Jesus warns us, "And fear not them which kill the body, but are not able to kill the soul: but rather fear him which is able to destroy both soul and body in hell."

Yes, there are many questions remaining, but the question as to whether or not Timothy McVeigh remains an agnostic is not among them.

IT DEPENDS UPON
WHAT "TRUTH" IS

People often travel to the ends of the earth, searching for "the truth." Some climb mountains to ask some old sage for the answer. Others try to descend deep into their consciousness to find the truth.

Many philosophies supposedly based on "the truth" only create confusion. Some say that there are different versions of the truth. Pure, unadulterated truth is considered either non-existent or a great mystery. Deliberate distortion of the principle of moral absolutes by agenda-led people lead many to believe that right is not always right and wrong may not be truly wrong. Each set of circumstances dictates its own truth. This is called moral relativity, or changeable truth.

Situational ethics says that stealing may be wrong for one person, but okay for another. If a liar has honorable intentions, he is not really lying. Symbolism is more important than substance. Meaning well is just as important as following through. Feeling someone else's pain (even if you caused the pain) means more than actually doing something to alleviate the pain.

Values clarification encourages each person to decide whether to establish, embrace, or reject principles and values for himself. Originally, values were based upon the words and meaning embodied in the Ten Commandments. Today, since the Commandments have been virtually outlawed, "values" is usually a word that people use to feign sincerity and empathy for others when none actually exists.

Is God's road map so secret that we must blindly fumble through life, hoping to chance upon the right path? Or are we to trust that by outweighing our bad with good deeds, we will attain whatever prize awaits us? Are ethics and morals truly circumstantial, or do absolutes clearly differentiate between right and wrong?

Some believe they should study all religions in order to fortify their own Christian walk. This may be a dangerous deception. Rather than finding truth through this method, they may find only confusion.

Has God provided the perfect plan for leading a fulfilled life here on earth? His Ten Commandments clearly explain what our relationship to Him and to others should be. The Scriptures are full of admonishments, rules, commands, and tips from our Creator that, if carefully followed, will dramatically increase our health, wealth, and overall happiness during our time on earth.

But, still, there seem to be situations that are so nebulous or complicated that they defy categorizing as clearly right or wrong. To further confuse us, there are plenty of false teachers, preachers, "channelers," and other charlatans ready to provide a humanistic, self-fulfilling, distorted, or even evil solutions to any spiritual or social question we may face.

Jesus advises His followers, in a passage often misused in order to justify gossip or slander, "If you abide in My word, you are my disciples indeed. And you shall know the truth, and the truth shall make you free" (John 8:32). In its true context, it tells us that we can know the truth in God's truth, as revealed by Christ through the word. Trying to determine the truth without knowing and abiding in Christ is futile.

The Bible is the final authority in determining truth. Apply each situation to God's standard, and confusion is avoided. Truth prevails. Hold every circumstance up against God's word and the truth stands out. But when God's word is distorted by man's logic, the truth is victimized. Likewise, when God's word is totally ignored or replaced with human understanding, the truth is lost.

We can know (abide in) God's heart through His word. He offers the free gift of eternal life through His Son, and an abundant life now. Counterfeit philosophies and distortions of the truth stand out like a sore thumb when viewed through the light of truth that is God's Word.

MENTORING YOUTH WORKS; "RACE POINTS" HURT.

Many university and black leaders complain that Michigan voters ended Affirmative Action in the November 2006 election. Many even threatened to ignore the public mandate. I, for one, am thankful that Michigan's voters curbed the destructive path these well-meaning administrators were following.

The vote stopped medical law schools from giving extra points toward entry to minority applicants. Academically qualified students were denied entry in favor of other, often academically deficient applicants simply because of skin color.

These programs actually hurt those they were trying to assist, because there is no evidence that anyone bothered to track the graduation rates of those given "race points." Black leaders seem to define "success" as increasing the numbers of black faces entering the programs while ignoring the dismal graduation rates of those who were given extra points. I requested data reflecting graduation rates of those provided extra points, and was advised that such data was not readily available.

If success is defined as an increase in the numbers of black entrants, with no regard to the fact that a majority of them wash out, then the program is a farce and should have been ended by the voters. The vote did not end Affirmative Action. State and federal laws still stand. It merely returned Affirmative Action to its original intent.

As a state administrator, I helped implement Michigan's Affirmative Action laws during the 1970s. The laws required those involved in hiring to affirmatively seek qualified applicants from protected and non-protected classes.

After making all reasonable efforts to obtain a representative pool of qualified candidates, fair and equitable interviews and exams were to be conducted, and the most qualified person was then selected. If done correctly, the numbers would take care of themselves.

Affirmative Action worked for me in the early 70s. After earning scores of 97%, 99 % and 100% on three state exams, I could not get an interview. I found that certain state agencies were hiring for positions for which I had passed tests. I presented my test scores and resume to the Personnel Managers in question, and was offered a position. My application had been "inadvertently overlooked." When Affirmative Action laws were later enacted, I was glad to see that, by law, the occurrence of "overlooked" qualified applicants would be greatly reduced.

Affirmative Action was never intended to give an unfair advantage to one group over another, but, throughout the years, many well-meaning people decided to give extra points based on race to increase the numbers of minorities in certain jobs and colleges. But, as previously stated, little interest was shown in determining success rates. That lack of interest in the outcomes of those given unfair "skin points" is, in itself, rather telling.

The administrators and "leaders" who push quota programs would be more effective if they spent time and resources to work on young children, helping them avoid bad role models and self-destructive behavior. Blacks often claim that, when a black male baby is born, a prison cell is built with his name on it, and that black youth are set up for failure by society. I respond that parents who neglect to train their children, give them a moral compass, and encourage excellence, while ignoring and/or excusing bad behavior are the ones who are building prison cells for their children. The Proverbial admonition, "Train a child in the way he should go, and when he is old he will not turn from it," stands as proven truth.

As to those who considered refusing to implement the new law, this is a dangerous concept to promote. If a group of people dislike the way the gubernatorial or legislative races turned out, should we refuse to allow the winners to be sworn in? It would be better for society as a whole if we all spent more time mentoring and discipling youth than dreaming up failure-ridden "remedies" later.

TURKEY DAY AND OTHER
DANGEROUS DECEPTIONS

Thanksgiving Day is often called "Turkey Day," and is usually spent hunting, eating, and watching sports. Few families use this holiday for what it was originally intended; to give thanks for our many blessings. Beginning in the Garden of Eden, humans have readily embraced many deceptions, and the replacement of the tradition of offering a day of thanks with a corny name and various activities and is clearly the result of deception.

Honoring the traditional Thanksgiving dinner entree rather than the One who provided the feast is considered, at worst, harmless fun. Labeling the day "Turkey Day" may trivialize what was created to be a thoughtful and solemn day of thanks for all of our blessings. We should not only set aside a special day, but should exhibit thankfulness every day, particularly those of us who were privileged to be born free in America, the world's most sought-after country of residence.

We truly have much to be thankful for. Giving thanks to our Creator does more for us than it does for God. He doesn't need our thanks. God provides for our needs, sending rain and sunshine to those who love Him and those who hate Him, alike. Being thankful reminds us of the many undeserved blessings we receive, but seldom acknowledge.

Our abandonment of thankfulness and honoring God has emboldened those who hate Him and His principles for living. Anti-God forces have become incrementally bolder in their agenda over the years. During the 1960s, they declared, "God is Dead!" then cowered for a time, awaiting a lightning bolt out of the blue. Nothing happened, so the next step was the vilification of the church, defining the so-called "Religious Right" as an entity to be feared; unwelcome in the public discourse. No lightning bolts struck, so the next step was total blasphemy. So-called artists use symbols of Christian religion in disgusting ways. It's open season on anything Christian. Christian symbols are desecrated with impunity, while humanistic, often evil symbols are provided Constitutional protection.

Perhaps it is simply human nature to believe that prosperity is totally a result of our own ingenuity and enlightened spirit, rather than of divine Providence. Many people dismiss any talk of a day of reckoning or the need to repent of sins. Such "old fashioned" concepts (worship, prayer, repentance, forgiveness) are often viewed as crutches for the weak or fodder for bad jokes. But those who believe that God is no longer in the business of dealing swiftly and directly with our animosity toward him should think again.

For many decades, the USSR was a powerful, atheistic empire which conquered and absorbed other nations with impunity. After years of conquest or intimidation of much of the world (with the exception of the U.S., which kept them pretty much in check), and blatant defiance of God's principles, the USSR arrogantly declared that God doesn't exist. God, in His infinite wisdom, apparently turned the tables on the great Soviet Union. While there are innumerable evidences of and testimonials to God's existence, no world map published in the past ten years makes any mention of the USSR, thereby declaring that the USSR is dead!

In Leviticus 26, God warns, "And, if you walk contrary to me, and are not willing to obey me, I will bring on you seven times more plagues…" He then lists examples of the despair he bring upon those who hate Him and despise His Word. Prosperous and powerful America should take heed and show thankfulness to God while we still can, and teach our young to fear and love the Lord, who offers abundant life on earth and eternal life through Christ to those who give Him the glory. The proper greeting is not "Happy Turkey Day," but "Have a blessed Thanksgiving Day!"

DO WE REALLY WANT A SOCIETY OF LIES AND TWISTED TRUTHS?

Some call the new millennium "The Age of Enlightenment." Most people have more information than ever about social trends, politics, etc. At the same time, we seem to be more gullible than ever.

An example of this was the quiet acceptance of assertions such as that of Kevorkian attorney Geoffrey Feiger, who said that Dr. Jack's patients did not die, they simply overcame their suffering. Today, vilifying people and twisting their words are the norm. We are told that our Founding Fathers wanted freedom from religion rather than freedom "of" religion, and that Dr. Martin Luther King, Jr., fought for welfare, excused blacks for bad behavior, and believed skin color is more relevant than good character.

Why do we enlightened people so willingly accept lies or twisted truths? Maybe in all of our enlightenment and political correctness, we are more likely to blindly follow those who say what we want to hear or who promise not to hold us accountable if we reciprocate.

U.S. history isn't taught effectively, so it is easy to convince many that the founders were, at best, agnostic. Many Americans are too intellectually lazy to research history to find out for themselves what the founders felt about religion, or to learn from Dr. King's own words that he promoted equal access and believed that the content of one's character is more important than the color of one's skin.

Yet, many buy the lies that distort his teachings and further an agenda that largely keeps Blacks poor and ignorant and therefore ineligible for good jobs. The lies also provide a large pool of victims through whom many leaders enrich themselves.

Politicians often lie about big oil, big business, and tax cuts for the wealthy. Class warfare is used to blame corporate America for problems, while giving industry no credit for our prosperity. Those who pay few taxes feel victimized by those who create jobs and wealth. Those with hidden agendas know that as long as we accept what we're told and refuse to stand for the truth we will increasingly fall for anything.

A current lie is the comparison of "The Christian Right" to the Taliban in Afghanistan, which criminalized teaching and learning, repressing their people through ignorance and fear. They murdered violators of their strict interpretation of their religious beliefs. To my knowledge, no Christian group in America has gone that far.

But, sadly, the dumbing down of America has rendered many Americans incapable of free thinking, and leads them to blindly follow whoever is the more strong-willed. Political correctness and other group-think concepts force the weak to fall into line. Our schools exacerbate the problem by focusing on and encouraging dangerous behavior and life choices and offering steps to avoid the consequences rather than teaching integrity, chastity, and appropriate life choices. Instead, the Ten Commandments are considered too dangerous to post in public places.

Many black leaders are intellectually dishonest when they blame bad behavior and delinquency on racism, the rich, or society, while overlooking black on black crime. They guard against bigotry while promoting reverse bigotry. True leaders would insist that people abandon dangerous life choices and lead exemplary lives themselves by avoiding sinful life choices, such as fathering children in adulterous relationships.

The Boy Scouts of America have been labeled bigots because people diametrically opposed to their century-old moral stance want to be placed in leadership positions. This honorable, wholesome segment of Americana has not changed its charter, yet the lie flourishes.

This dangerous trend of twisting the truth for personal gain may, indeed, explain the staunch resistance against posting the Ten Commandments in public. Could the one against "bearing false witness against one's neighbor" be one of the most feared?

WHO HOLDS THE KEY TO
OUR SOCIAL MORASS?

Many Americans express concern about the lack of family values, declining morals, lack of empathy for others, and other spiritual problems that plague us as a nation. Many people believe they have the key to resolving such challenges. Keys like more love, or more money or more government programs are offered. Others don't see anything appreciably wrong. The problems are simply a sign of the times.

Concern about such issues often leads people to become introspective, asking what they can do to alleviate the problems. Profound-sounding mantras are spoken, such as, "If it is to be, it must begin with me!"

Such bold statements are usually uttered by someone who is on a crusade to help the less fortunate. The underlying causes of poverty are often internal and self-inflicted, and therefore, not easily resolved by well-meaning crusaders. Personal responsibility and self-discipline are goals that will render the person a better future. Someone said that everyone wants to change the world, but no one is willing to change his own heart.

The primary causes of our spiritual and moral morass are more personal than societal. If concerned Americans are to return this nation to its moral beginnings and, thereby to the blessings of a nation whose God is the Lord, it will not begin with meetings, marches, protests, or group therapy. It must begin within the heart of each person. The human condition renders us unable to be perfect or make perfect life choices. However, we are to strive for excellence; to reach the highest level of morality possible, and make repentance and prayer the focus of life. Otherwise, we merely aim for the dregs of life, where anything goes and life is meaningless and unfulfilled.

A person who does not first put his life in proper order is ill-prepared to assist anyone else in overcoming destructive, immoral behavior. Each succeeding generation of youth seems to be viler than the previous one, while parents are increasingly unable or unwilling to correct bad behavior. Parents who never had self-discipline in their own lives certainly cannot impart such attributes to their children. How can a parent expect a child to act appropriately who has no relationship with (or knowledge of) the one who wrote the moral code? And a child who sees little or no discipline, honesty or prayer in his parents' lives won't strive for self-control or seek answers in prayer.

Each person must purpose to live a chaste life, complete with prayer and meditation. In the Bible, we are told to, "... [cast] down arguments and every high thing that exalts itself against the knowledge of God, bringing every thought into captivity to the obedience of Christ." Then, and only then, can one begin to work on family, church and community problems.

Each one of us holds the key. We can give it benign neglect or use it by ordering our personal life in and living in obedience to Christ, who will, in return, provide the moral authority necessary to rid ourselves of moral and spiritual problems. Once we bring our own life into focus and under the authority of Christ, then we can be effective in helping others to rid themselves of destructive behavior. Christ is the key.

CREEPING KUDZU AND CREEPING COMPROMISE

They rose out of the ravine at twilight like giant, shrouded behemoths, some more than thirty feet high. Through the late summer fog, the wind made them appear to move toward me in slow motion. Fear and dread seized me by the throat, and my knees began to wobble, so I hurried back to my father-in-law's house before my mind got carried away. We were on vacation near Knoxville, Tennessee, in the foothills of the Great Smoky Mountains. When I told Dad what I had seen, he chuckled, "That's just Kudzu. I'll show you in the morning when the light is better."

After a restless night of pondering what I had seen, I peered out the bedroom window the next morning, half expecting to find the house covered in that green growth. Kudzu (cud- zoo) is a plant that was brought from Japan in the nineteenth century to control soil erosion, and as animal fodder. During the Depression, the U.S. Soil Conservation Service paid farmers to fill their fields with the Kudzu vine. Even though Kudzu has many useful purposes, it grows too well. By 1972, it was labeled a weed that can grow a foot each day, and sixty feet per year. It can take over fences, trees, telephone poles, and people have reported that it grows into homes through closed windows at night.

As I gazed out into the deep ravine, the sight literally took my breath away. The trees were so completely covered with leafy green vines that the branches were indistinguishable. They resembled the botanical designs by Edward Scissorhands. Jutting up here and there in the midst of the trees were bare wooden spikes that used to be trees. Kudzu's covering shuts out light and moisture, killing any live thing in its path.

My in-laws' neighbor, Mr. Buford, is waging a war against the vine, mowing his property along the edge of the ravine sometimes three times a day. The kudzu simply started to grow straight up, forming a five-foot "fence" in defiance of Buford's efforts to hold it at bay. But Buford is undaunted. He has accepted the challenge and goes about methodically each and every day.

He said that the government tried to kill it with herbicides, but that only made it grow more. What's worse, Kudzu is perennial. It dies off each winter and grows back stronger than ever each spring. Mr. Buford said that for years they were told that Kudzu could never live in northern Tennessee because the frost would kill it. He didn't believe it could travel much further up north because the winters are harsher in Kentucky and Ohio, but he is determined that it won't advance on his watch. As we traveled home to Michigan, we saw Kudzu growing defiantly as far as the middle part of Kentucky.

Kudzu is like many social and cultural crusades that begin with good intentions, only to be taken so far to the extreme that the bad outpaces the good, rendering the effort more detrimental than helpful. Kudzu could be compared to the many programs and policies that began with good intentions, but, in the end, caused more problems than they resolved. In a world of complacency and apathy people don't see the dangers that accompany radical changes in ethics and morals. Compromise rules the day, creeping along and devouring unsuspecting people who think themselves "enlightened." Kudzu could be compared to our sinful human nature, which constantly strives to control and defeat us. Only dedicated vigilance is effective in holding it at bay.

We who understand the dangers presented by compromise should take up the challenge to be Bufords, keeping these dangerous lapses in judgment from overtaking us all, raking and mowing them back with the truth of Scripture and culling the vines that try to sneak past our guard with prayer. God wants us to be Bufords in his cause. In Psalms 94:16, He asks, "Who will rise up for me against the workers of iniquity?" We have to become Bufords and stand up for what is right and true, according to God's Word, and continue to hold the line against the encroaching spread of immorality and apathy.

ASSISTED SUICIDE AND QUALITY OF LIFE

Matthew Johnson, a bright, athletic Minnesota twenty-five-year-old was the envy of his peers. He loved all sports and was well on his way to his dream career as a professional power lifter ... until he was paralyzed from the neck down in a moto-cross accident in the summer of 1997. On a January night in 1998, Matt's body was dropped off outside Detroit's Beaumont Hospital.

Matt became the youngest person, to date, to avail himself of the services of Jack Kevorkian. The doctor supposedly catered only to the old, infirm, terminal, and pain-wracked. Matt had none of these complaints, but he shared one lament with Kevorkian's other "clients," the lack of "quality of life." Matt's family said that although Matt's injury was not life-threatening, he couldn't cope with not having "quality" in his life. This worn-out phrase is used to justify everything from lack of initiative to, well, death. Quality of life is defined today as being able to do everything one wants in life with few, if any, limitations and zero adversity or consequences. In the Netherlands, where euthanasia is legal, many people, including kids with birth defects are euthanized because they face no "quality of life."

Just what is quality of life? If it is a by-product of personal achievement and reaching the pinnacle of one's field or sport, then why are those who reach such lofty heights so often unfulfilled and sad? In fact, many people have found true quality in life only after severe adversity had changed their lives drastically and destroyed any chance of achieving the excellence they had targeted for themselves.

For instance, teenager Joni Eareckson-Tada broke her neck in a diving accident. Instead of feeling sorry for herself, she became a singer, writer, painter, and motivational speaker, all while confined to a wheelchair, paralyzed from the neck down. She has discovered true quality of life. The late actor Christopher Reeve became paralyzed in a fall from a horse. Until his death, he trusted that science would discover treatment that would allow him to walk again, but, he did not sit in the dark, nursing despair. He spoke to other paraplegics, encouraging them to find fulfillment within the limitations of their conditions. He has even starred in the remake of *Rear Window*. His life is changed, but not diminished by his condition. He and his wife, Dana founded the Christopher and Dana Reeve Foundation to help others with paralyzing conditions. Dana continued working with the foundation until her husband's death.

Lesser known Mike Edwards lost a leg to cancer as a child, but he set a goal of playing basketball for Notre Dame University. Through faith and diligence, he realized his goal and joined the 1998 Notre Dame Basketball team, and has seen significant playing time for a freshman. His friends say that, throughout his life, Mike has always spent more time caring about others than worrying about his own problems or setbacks. His quality of life stems from helping others.

It seems that many of those who rise above the despair of major adversity are the ones who change their focus from their own goals and dreams to finding ways to help others. When we begin to look outside ourselves for satisfaction and gratification, and search for ways to serve others, even a debilitating injury or physical problem cannot destroy our sense of worth. When my Aunt Bessie, who reared my nine siblings and me after we were orphaned, lay wracked by excruciating pain from stomach and bone cancer, she didn't pray for death; she prayed for us, and, right up to the end, she taught and encouraged us. She had the key to quality of life. The key is love. One of her favorite biblical characters was Job, who lost his family and possessions, and sat in the ashes of his world. Encouraged by others to mock God for allowing such ruination Job, instead declared, "Though He slay me, yet will I trust Him" (Job 3:13). Quality of life, for Job and for my aunt, was defined as love and trust in the Lord.

When we love others as ourselves, as we are instructed to do throughout the Bible, we focus on what we can do for them rather than what we can achieve for ourselves. True love, true satisfaction comes from showing the love of God to others. Paul tells us, "...but now abide faith, hope, love...but the greatest of these is love" (1 Cor. 13:13). Love based in faith and hope is capable of healing from the heart out.

DREADING THE NEXT
TRAIN WRECK

We've all watched movie scenes in which an out of control train crashes, in slow motion, into a vehicle, a train station wall, another train, etc. Such imagery is often used to describe the self-destructive actions of a person, such as a celebrity, who makes choices that put him on course toward a deadly collision. What's more terrifying is the way our impressionable youth and others adore such celebrities.

We saw it with Anna Nicole Smith, who seemed to "have it all," but died of what has been described as a drug overdose in a Florida casino. Anna didn't descend into the depths of drug abuse quietly and without witnesses. No, she was often seen in public in a drugged stupor. She even starred in her own TV program, shamelessly flaunting her severely dysfunctional life for all to see.

Although Anna's drug and alcohol issues were widely known, those close to her felt no urgency to beg her to stop. After her death, many people came forward to describe how they watched her destroy herself without so much as a whimper of protest. Anna left behind a baby girl, embroiled in a battle to establish her paternity, and a reputation that can only be described as shameful.

People today idolize "stars" for all the wrong reasons. Anna Nicole Smith was worshipped for her looks and low-life persona. Britney Spears, Paris Hilton, and Lindsay Lohan are current train wrecks waiting to happen. They constantly act out in dangerous ways, yet they are worshipped and cheered. They should be pitied. People such as these are usually very sad and unhappy inside. They know better than anyone just how superficial and empty their lives are outside of the media spotlight.

Two rappers, Ja Rule and 'Lil' Wayne, were recently arrested for drug and gun violations, one while driving his $400,000 luxury car. At one time, such activity would have opened both celebrities to ridicule and a loss of audience, but, in today's misplaced affection and admiration, both of these "artists" can expect a significant boost in their popularity. Kids will continue to buy and play their CDs, and their producers will continue to crank out the filth they call music.

Today, it seems that everything has been turned on its head. Good is bad, wrong is right; bad behavior is rewarded, and criminals and miscreants are honored and revered. Proper behavior and the pursuit of excellence, on the other hand, are ridiculed and castigated as silly. We have been so blessed and have obtained and achieved so much as a society that we seem to have forgotten the source of our gains.

God set forth rules by which we are to order our lives. We have free will to operate outside of those parameters and set our own standards of right and wrong, sometimes without immediate consequences. But, consequences are evident everywhere, although we seldom connect the dots. Often, the consequences are sudden, brutal, and final, such as with Anna Nicole, who died suddenly and disgracefully. Sometimes consequences are ignored, as with Paris Hilton, who, after a much publicized stint in jail, is up to her old tricks.

While many people dream of trading places with celebrities, the stars themselves, are often acting out in a cry for help, as in the old movie line, " ... Somebody *stop* me!" Sadly, more often than not, nobody does, until it's too late. Many parents allow their children to worship and emulate such people, and then find themselves at a loss as to how to help youngsters deal with the inevitable consequences.

The minds of children and others who have refused to learn what God says about such lifestyles can be easily duped into thinking that such self-destructive life choices are something to be desired. We should strive to teach our youth that guidelines given by God, such as leading a chaste and honorable life, and avoiding destructive people and substances, are the only keys to a long, prosperous and fulfilled life. From the outside looking in, the fast life looks ideal, but we are warned in Proverbs 14:12, "There is a way that seems right (to mankind), but in the end it leads to death."

ARE GOOD SAMARITANS CREATED BY LAW OR PERSONAL ETHICS?

Many states have Good Samaritan laws that require people to aid victims. In Biblical times, the Samaritans and the Jews hated each other. Jesus told a parable in which a Samaritan stopped to aid a Jewish traveler who had been attacked and beaten by bandits. The Samaritan bandaged the man and paid for a room for the victim in an inn (Luke 10:33–37).

In a Las Vegas casino bathroom, Jeremy Strohmeyer, nineteen, raped and murdered a seven-year-old girl. His friend, David Cash, witnessed the hideous crime, but failed to intervene or report the attack. The two men then rode roller coasters all night. Nevada wants to make it a crime to fail to report or intervene in a crime in progress, unless personal harm is likely, in which case the incident must be reported immediately.

David Cash enrolled at the University of California at Berkley. Students and faculty alike were outraged that a person with such blatant disregard for human life was allowed to enroll. But college officials insisted that he had a right to attend. In a TV interview, Cash defiantly explained that he had no responsibility to help the girl because he didn't know her, and, "She wasn't anything to me."

Cash's attitude is not new. In Genesis, God, aware that Cain had killed his brother, asked him where Abel was. Cain answered, "I do not know. Am I my brother's keeper?" Does God expect us to aid victims of crime or misfortune? Would most people have at least tried to stop Strohmeyer, or reported the crime to save the girl?

Strohmeyer is facing the death penalty. He and Cash may face an even worse fate than that. God is very expressive about His love for children. In Matthew 18:10, Jesus warns, "Take heed that you do not despise one of these little ones, for I say to you that in heaven their angels see the face of my Father who is in heaven." Is such apathy so prevalent in society today because many people no longer know or care what God says, or is it simply selfishness to the extreme?

People rarely take the opportunity to be a Good Samaritan today, sometimes because of fear of being attacked, themselves, and sometimes out of pure apathy. Today, people just don't want to get involved in the problems of others. TV talk show (trash show) guests brag about their mistreatment of and callous disregard for others, when their actions should cause them to hide in shame. Videos and movies glamorize wolf-pack predatory acts against the weak, while depicting moral living as comical, outdated, and boring. It makes one shudder to think that many of today's children have no moral training or compass, and are growing into future Strohmeyers and Cashs.

Could these miscreants have missed some critical lessons from those who reared them? A father in Proverbs obviously knew that his son tended to be a follower, and was willing to guide his child. He warned, "My son, if sinners entice you, do not consent. If they say, 'come with us. Let us lie in wait to shed blood; let us lurk secretly for the innocent without cause'…My son, do not walk in the way with them…"

Many parents today prefer to be friends with their children than to teach them to live moral and chaste lives. As a result, many of our youth are free-falling unchecked down the slippery slope of self-destruction, into the valley of crime, drugs, homicide, and even death, while society "protects" them by helping them avoid the consequences of bad behavior. The so-called "Religious Right" is construed to be more dangerous to children than drugs, even though it clearly espouses principles that are proven to bring about positive change.

It is incumbent upon parents and churches to take back the job of rearing their young. We are our brothers' keeper, and God expects us to love our children enough to bring them under the authority of all that Christ taught us—not because man's law ordains it, but because God commanded it; "…you shall love your neighbor as yourself…" (Lev. 19:18).

IS INTEGRITY THE
MISSING INGREDIENT?

Today, people like to categorize and rate misbehavior. (Is what Michael Vick did as bad as what Larry Craig did? Is Louisiana Congressman Jefferson having $90,000 in marked money in his freezer as bad as Senator Vitter's name showing up in the telephone records of a Washington madam?)

Comparison is odious. It may be more useful to discuss why successful people take reckless chances with their reputation, job, and future. If a person cannot shake serious character flaws, then why risk one's reputation by taking those flaws with them into high-profile positions?

We constantly see people in sports, entertainment and politics participating in foolish, dangerous and sometimes self-destructive activities. The reactions to such public bad behavior range from smugness in watching someone fall off the pedestal we've placed them on, to shock, to anger that someone would risk fame and fortune for some dead-end activity.

There was a time when people would take stock of themselves after being blessed with fortune or fame, and try

to remove from their life any characteristics, habits or activities that are counterproductive to their life goals. Nowadays, however, it seems that they believe they can carry self-destructive behavior right into the arena, and force those behaviors to fit where they do not belong.

A person who participates in such behaviors, especially one who is going into highly visible, high-profile areas such as politics, entertainment, sports, etc., should make a conscious decision to remove such elements from his live. Otherwise, he risks losing his position and status and tainting the institution. People of integrity tend to make the right decisions about self-destructive behavior. But, apparently, integrity is not often seen as an essential ingredient in seeking success.

Michael Vick reportedly has been involved in dog-fighting, gambling and other juvenile activities since his youth. When he was drafted into the NFL, one would think that he would strive to rid himself of these habits, perhaps in gratitude for the blessing of the wealth and fame offered by professional football. Now that he has lost untold millions in salary and endorsements, not to mention his reputation and honor, he declares that he has "found Jesus." Would that it be so. Too bad he neglected to look for Jesus when the Lord was standing at the door of his heart and knocking.

Senator Craig apparently has, for many years, been dogged with allegations of what newsman Chris Matthews calls "deviant behavior." The media and others tend to focus on the details of the misdeed, rather than the overall problem within the soul of the perpetrator. In God's eyes, it is sinful to have any sexual-type relations in public restrooms, be they hetero-sexual or homosexual. If Larry Craig knew that he had a propensity to involve himself in serious hidden

sin, he should not have entered into a position of public trust in the first place.

Many rappers follow the same pattern. Often deeply involved in gangs, drugs, and weapons offenses as teens, they simply carry such activities with them into stardom. Since rappers often incorporate dead-end themes into their "music," few are surprised when a rapper becomes involved in violence, drugs or other criminal activity. Unlike politicians and sports stars, some rappers don't even try to hide their deviant behavior. They celebrate it, and so do their sheep-like fans.

The Bible says that we are all sinners, and all manner of evil emanates from the heart of mankind. The only way to control our sinful nature is through the saving grace of Jesus Christ. If we refuse to surrender such sin areas to God, and fill our hearts with righteousness, we can only expect serious consequences, sooner or later. When those sin areas are exposed, we are left with ridicule and loss of standing in the minds of others.

In Corinthians, it says, "When I was a child, I talked like a child, I thought like a child, I reasoned like a child. When I became a man, I put childish ways behind me." To those who believe they can continue childish ways and lead double lives without being detected, God says, "...you may be sure that your sin will find you out." And shame and humiliation will surely follow.

ROLL CALL AT THE MILLSTONE FACTORY

It was the most horrific sight ever witnessed by mankind. A line of mournful people, stretching as far as the eye could see, moving rapidly, in single file into one end of a huge, dark, and menacing building. Each one briefly reappears from the other end with a large round cement stone chained around his neck. One by one, they fall, howling, into a fiery ocean at the bottom of an abyss.

Those approaching the building's entryway are unable to shake the damning scenes from their lives, being played over and over in their minds like a somber movie. They watch in horror as each reprobate suffers the doom that would soon face them all. Many of them clearly understand why they are about to suffer this terrifying, eternal ordeal. They now understand, although too late, the cost of their unrepentant life choices.

Those who had kidnapped and/or murdered children, or forced and coerced children into lives of crime and degradation had no plea. Those who neglected the children with whom they had been blessed by refusing to protect and guide

them were well aware that they had, in their selfishness, deliberately ignored the warnings about such activity.

Still others, however, felt they were being wrongfully punished. Some of them had really believed they were acting as advocates for children when they fought for children's "rights," such as the right to divorce themselves from or sue their parents for trying to parent them as best they could. Others were painfully aware that, they had, for profit or self-gratification led children into self-destructive lifestyles through evil music, immoral movies and fashion trends.

Those who had constantly complained about the plight of children, while fiercely promoting the "choice" to destroy children in the womb or after partial birth, and had refused to repent and turn away were shocked to find that it was now too late to make amends. Likewise, those who had perpetrated evil acts upon children without detection were now exposed to the light for all to see, and had to bear the guilt and shame of their lack of repentance before all people. Sound like a grotesque Spielberg movie? This fictionalization is very unlikely to ever take place, but the sobering truth about this scenario is that something much worse will most certainly take place.

Jesus warned that, "If anyone should cause one of these little ones to lose his faith in me, it would be better for that person to have a large millstone tied around his neck and be drowned in the deep sea." As chilling as the thought of countless people being dragged by cement neckties to the bottom of the ocean, Christ actually promises that such treatment would be better than what is actually in store for such people.

Daily, we hear hideous and heart-breaking stories of evil acts against children. Neglect runs rampant, and children are being placed in dangerous situations. Even child advocates often protect only those groups of children who enhance their agenda, while dispatching, with impunity, those who have no champion, or little political collateral.

In our human condition, we all sin and no parent can do everything right. God wants us to purpose to do right, rather than to choose to do wrong. This follows in rearing and protecting children as well as in all areas of life. For those who are sorry for their sins and shortcomings, God offers an unconditional pardon through His Son, who has already paid the price for all sin.

Unrepentance is the same as refusing to acknowledge that one has sinned against God. He repeatedly warns us of the penalty for disobedience and lack of repentance, but some of His strongest warnings are to those who take advantage of His beloved children.

We pray that many will see themselves as God sees them, and come to a place where they understand their need for a Savior. And may those who harm or allow harm to children come to repentance.

A JOB WELL DONE, GOOD
AND FAITHFUL SERVANT

Steadfast Christians are often called "prayer warriors." One great warrior was Dr. D. James Kennedy. He triumphantly entered Heaven on September 5, 2007, not because he killed his enemies or performed good works, but because he trusted in Jesus Christ alone for his salvation. He now has the free gift of eternal life because of the suffering, death and resurrection of Jesus Christ.

CNN's Christiane Amanpour recently did a special report, "God's Warriors," comparing religious militancy among the three major religions of Islam, Judaism, and Christianity. It seemed to attempt to prove that adherents of all three religions are equally zealous in their battle against their enemies.

The report seems to indicate (but fails to prove) that there is little or no difference between jihadists, who destroy innocent life (and themselves), and who seek the destruction of enemy nations; Israel (which lives in a defensive posture against many nations sworn to destroy it); and Christians, whose God tells us to love our enemies. The show seemed to opine that making inflammatory statements (as Jerry Falwell, Pat Robertson and others may have done on occasion) is the same as the killing of innocents. Apparently, the producers of this program have little knowledge of true Christians or the One we follow.

In many religions, believers must perform many works, rituals and pilgrimages, and convert or kill unbelievers to "earn" paradise. The Bible teaches that God gives us the faith to believe, through His Holy Spirit, and saves us through the blood and sacrifice of His Son, Jesus Christ. God does not need us to fight His battles. We wage war against evil through prayer. Songs such as "Onward Christian Soldiers" mention war, only to reveal that Christ is our defender and has already won the victory. We can only receive or reject the victory that has already been won for us.

Ephesians tells us that the war against evil is not a struggle "... against flesh and blood, but against the evil rulers, powers and forces in the heavenly realms..." We don't have to physically fight the enemy. Instead we are to "... put on the whole armor of God, so that when evil comes, you may be able to stand your ground...." This is accomplished by placing the "... belt of truth around our waist, and the breastplates of righteousness in place; taking up the shield of faith," the sword of the Spirit and the helmet of salvation.

So, while many religions spend all of their time waging a world-wide battle to turn the world to their way of thinking, the Bible teaches us that Jesus Christ has already vanquished evil. In the song "A Mighty Fortress is our God," taken from Psalms 46, we are reminded that we have a champion, who "... holds the field forever..." Therefore, the overall battle between good and evil is already won by Jesus Christ, our champion and redeemer, who has defeated death to show us the way to eternal life. He will return and take to Himself those who trust in Him alone for salvation and eternal life. Those who have rejected His free gift, along with Satan, will be cast into the sea of fire forever.

God never required Dr. Kennedy to attack his enemies, yet he "fought the good fight," as the Bible commands us to do—not with physical strength, but with inspiration from the Holy Spirit. He commands us to go and tell others about the saving, undeserved grace of God. Dr. Kennedy didn't attack other religions. He spent his life sharing and training others to share the truth of the Holy Scriptures, through the power of God's unerring Word.

The CNN special, then, fails in its attempt to bring Christianity down to the level of humanistic religions. Unlike other "religions," Christianity does not depend on mortals to fight or defeat our enemies. God knew better than we that all mankind are hopeless, doomed sinners and cannot save ourselves. In His love for His creation, He prepared the only way to forgiveness and everlasting life: His son, Jesus Christ. We don't need to wage Holy war. Instead we pray for our enemies, because the battle has already been won!